# Continuous Permanent Improvement

Also available from ASQ Quality Press:

*Process Improvement Simplified: A How-to Book for Success in Any Organization*
James B. King, Francis G. King, and Michael W. R. Davis

*Business Process Improvement Toolbox*, Second Edition
Bjørn Andersen

*The Quality Toolbox*, Second Edition
Nancy R. Tague

*Mapping Work Processes*, Second Edition
Bjørn Andersen, Tom Natland Fagerhaug, Bjørnar Henriksen, and Lars E. Onsøyen

*The ASQ Quality Improvement Pocket Guide: Basic History, Concepts, Tools, and Relationships*
Grace L. Duffy, editor

*Performance Metrics: The Levers for Process Management*
Duke Okes

*The Executive Guide to Innovation: Turning Good Ideas into Great Results*
Jane Keathley, Peter Merrill, Tracy Owens, Ian Meggarrey, and Kevin Posey

*Outcomes, Performance, Structure (OPS): Three Keys to Organizational Excellence*
Michael E. Gallery and Stephen C. Carey

*The ASQ Pocket Guide for the Certified Six Sigma Black Belt*
T. M. Kubiak

*The ASQ Pocket Guide to Root Cause Analysis*
Bjørn Andersen and Tom Natland Fagerhaug

*The Quality Improvement Handbook*, Second Edition
ASQ Quality Management Division and John E. Bauer, Grace L. Duffy, Russell T. Westcott, editors

*Process Improvement Using Six Sigma: A DMAIC Guide*
Rama Shankar

*The Certified Manager of Quality/Organizational Excellence Handbook,*
Fourth Edition
Russell T. Westcott, editor

To request a complimentary catalog of ASQ Quality Press publications, call 800-248-1946, or visit our website at www.asq.org/quality-press.

# Continuous Permanent Improvement

Arun Hariharan

*Forewords by Mikel J. Harry, PhD
and Dr. Kewal K. Nohria*

ASQ Quality Press
Milwaukee, Wisconsin

American Society for Quality, Quality Press, Milwaukee 53203
© 2014 by ASQ
All rights reserved. Published 2014
Printed in the United States of America
20 19 18 17 16 15 14    5 4 3 2 1

**Library of Congress Cataloging-in-Publication Data**

Hariharan, Arun.
  Continuous permanent improvement / Arun Hariharan ; forewords by Mikel J. Harry, Ph.D. and Dr. Kewal K. Nohria.
     pages cm
  Includes bibliographical references and index.
  ISBN 978-0-87389-886-7 (hardcover : alk. paper)
  1. Total quality management. 2. Organizational effectiveness. 3. Quality assurance. 4. Success in business. I. Title.

  HD62.15.H365 2014
  658.4'013—dc23                                                              2014010125

ISBN 978-0-87389-886-7

No part of this book may be reproduced in any form or by any means, electronic, mechanical, photocopying, recording, or otherwise, without the prior written permission of the publisher.

Acquisitions Editor: Matt T. Meinholz
Managing Editor: Paul Daniel O'Mara
Production Administrator: Randall Benson

ASQ Mission: The American Society for Quality advances individual, organizational, and community excellence worldwide through learning, quality improvement, and knowledge exchange.

Attention Bookstores, Wholesalers, Schools, and Corporations: ASQ Quality Press books, video, audio, and software are available at quantity discounts with bulk purchases for business, educational, or instructional use. For information, please contact ASQ Quality Press at 800-248-1946, or write to ASQ Quality Press, P.O. Box 3005, Milwaukee, WI 53201-3005.

To place orders or to request ASQ membership information, call 800-248-1946. Visit our website at http://www.asq.org/quality-press.

 Printed on acid-free paper

Quality Press
600 N. Plankinton Ave.
Milwaukee, WI 53203-2914
E-mail: authors@asq.org

**The Global Voice of Quality™**

*To my parents Lakshmi and N. A. Hariharan,
my wife Bhuvana, our children Lakshmi and Srihari,
and to all the quality masters.*

# Table of Contents

List of Figures and Tables .................................. xiii
Foreword by Mikel J. Harry, PhD ......................... xv
Foreword by Dr. Kewal K. Nohria ......................... xvi
Preface ........................................................ xvii

**Chapter 1  Business or Excellence: Do We Have a Choice?** ........................................... 1
   Aiming for Leadership—Fast ........................... 1
   Growing Pains ............................................. 2
   Mad About Growth ....................................... 2
   An Expensive Lesson .................................... 3

**Chapter 2  Make Quality Your Strategy** .............. 5
   Know Where You Want to Go and How to Get There ... 6
   Do You Have a Business Excellence Road Map? ....... 11

**Chapter 3  Whose Job Is Excellence?** ................. 17
   Do Boards Represent Customers Enough? ............ 18
   Questions That the Board Must Ask .................. 18
   How to Ensure That the Board Doesn't Get into Too Much Detail ........................................... 19
   Why Can't One Director Represent the Customer as a Key Stakeholder? ................................... 19
   Why the Board Must Ask These Questions ........... 20
   Indicators of Organizations Where the Board Focuses on Quality and Customers ......................... 20
   The CEO's Role ........................................... 21
   Chicken and Egg .......................................... 22
   Excellence Is Everyone's Job ........................... 23
   Is Quality the Job of the "Quality Department"? ..... 23

## Chapter 4  Begin from the Beginning: Know Who Your Customers Are and What They Want ............ 25
SIPOC and COPIS.................................... 27
COPIS as a Strategy ................................ 27
What Type of Business or Organization Is This Relevant To?....................................... 28
The Story of How Strategic COPIS Was Applied ....... 29
Keeping Processes and Performance Measures Current ........................................... 35
Is It Relevant Only in a New Business?............... 35
Foundation for Continuous Improvement ............. 37
Business Benefits of Strategic COPIS................. 38
Output of Strategic COPIS: Master List of Business Processes........................................ 39
Conclusion......................................... 41

## Chapter 5  Standardize to Improve: Business Process Mapping ................................. 43
Grandma Cakes..................................... 43
Explosive Growth—the Artisan Multiplies Herself ..... 44
Standardized Business Processes .................... 45
*Who* Needs Standardized Business Processes?......... 46
The Process Map.................................... 46
Do Standardized Processes Kill Innovation? On the Contrary .................................... 52
Why Do You Need Standardized Processes? .......... 54
You Can Have Your Own Format for Process Mapping ......................................... 54
Who Should Document Processes?................... 55
How Do You Know If People Are Following the Standard Process?................................ 56
The Role of Automation and the Need for Wing-to-Wing Thinking .................................. 57
Conclusion......................................... 58

## Chapter 6  Measures That Matter .................... 59
Two Years Later..................................... 66
The Dashboard Review .............................. 67

## Chapter 7  The Beginning of Improvement: Making Quality Problems Visible ......................... 71
Measurement Itself Causes Improvement ............. 72

Where to Begin Improvement—Start by Making
   Quality Problems Visible ..................... 72
Clear the Cobwebs with 5S ...................... 74
Listen to Customer Complaints and Look at Your
   Performance Measures ........................ 75

**Chapter 8   The Fascinating World of Lean ............ 77**
Lean Is for Senior Management First ............... 77
Identifying and Eliminating Waste (the Nine Types
   of Waste)..................................... 78
What We Learned from Toyota..................... 82
Value Stream Mapping—Autobiography of a Sales
   Order ........................................ 83
Is This Value? ................................... 86
The Invisible Mountain ........................... 88
Value Stream Mapping Makes the Mountain of Waste
   Visible ....................................... 89
You Have Started Winning the Battle Against Quality
   Problems and Waste .......................... 90
Examples of Fighting Waste and Results ............ 91
Lean Can Double Your Profits .................... 93
Is This Relevant in Service Industries?.............. 94
Involving Partners ............................... 95
Now That You Can See the Mountain, Demolish It!..... 96

**Chapter 9   Double Your Revenue and Profits
without Selling More: the Importance of First
Time Right ....................................... 97**
Why Is FTR So Important?....................... 97
FTR in Sales .................................... 99
What Is an FTR Sale?............................ 100
Where Is FTR Selling Relevant?................... 101
FTR and Cost of Rework......................... 101
FTR and Customer Satisfaction.................... 102
FTR and Company Image ........................ 102
The Impact of FTR on Revenue, Profits, and Sales
   Productivity................................... 103
Mental Blocks ................................... 104
Lesson Learned—Only Sales Must Be Responsible
   for FTR in Sales .............................. 105
How Do You Know If It's Working?................ 106
What You Can Do ............................... 106

## Chapter 10   A Management Philosophy Called Six Sigma .................................... 109
The Project Charter, and Reporting Results from
    Lean Six Sigma (LSS)......................... 114
Lean and Six Sigma—a Powerful Combination ........ 116
Three Types of Lean Six Sigma Projects ............. 117
    Quality Improvement Projects .................. 117
    Revenue-Enhancing Projects ................... 117
    Cost-Saving Projects ......................... 119
How to Select and Prioritize LSS Projects ........... 120
Do Not Marry a Model ........................... 120
What to Do When Customers Complain.............. 121

## Chapter 11   Is a Complaining Customer Doing You a Favor?..................................... 123
The Customer's Story ............................ 123
The Bank's Side of the Story...................... 124
The Bank's Story Six Months Later ................ 124
The Customer (as Always) Has the Last Word ........ 124

## Chapter 12   Resolved, but Not Resolved .............. 127
A Riddle ....................................... 127
At Last, Some Light.............................. 129
Other "Smart" Ways of Beating the System .......... 130
The Final Outcome .............................. 131
The Lesson ..................................... 131

## Chapter 13   Root Cause Analysis .................... 133
The Technique of Root Cause Analysis............... 136
Sample Business Results from Root Cause Analysis .... 138
Critical Success Factors—Lessons Learned in Root
    Cause Analysis ............................. 139
Tests to Find Out If You Have Reached the Root Cause
    and Eliminated It............................ 148
RCA—the Epitome of Lean ....................... 149
Can Problems Be Prevented *before* They Ever
    Occur?..................................... 150

## Chapter 14   Close the Loop with the Customer ........ 153
The Meeting with the CEO........................ 157
The Commandments (Lessons Learned) ............. 158
What's *Your* Company's Culture?................... 161

## Chapter 15 *Kaizen* and the Power of Ideas ............. 163
A Shaky Start .................................. 164
A Process for Ideas and Innovation—at Two Levels..... 165
Innovation Process for Large Business Ideas .......... 167
Continuous Process for Innovation ................. 168
Will Ideas Dry Up?............................. 169
Your Company's Culture Can Either Encourage or
  Kill Innovation .............................. 170
The Impact on People and Morale.................. 171
Conclusion..................................... 173

## Chapter 16   360-Degree Knowledge Management ...... 175
Introduction to the 360-Degree Knowledge
  Management Model........................... 176
*What* Is Knowledge Management? .................. 177
*Why* Knowledge Management?..................... 177
The Six *How* Questions........................... 177
Communities of Experts and Knowledge Champions.... 178
Role of Knowledge Champions and Communities
  of Experts .................................. 179
The First Three *How* Questions Have Been Answered... 179
*How* KM Really Works........................... 179
The 360-Degree Knowledge Management Model....... 180
The Six Dimensions of 360-Degree KM.............. 181
Balancing Relevance and Content Quality with
  Culture Building ............................. 184
Establish Standard KM Processes................... 185
The Role of Technology in 360-Degree KM........... 185
Examples of Business Results from Application of
  360-Degree KM .............................. 186
Knowledge-Dollars or K-Dollars.................... 187
Conclusion...................................... 187

## Chapter 17   Do Business Excellence Models Help?...... 189

## Chapter 18   A Word to Business Leaders ............. 193

## Chapter 19   A Word to Quality Professionals.......... 201

## Chapter 20   A Word to Services .................... 213

## Chapter 21   Summing Up: The Cycle of Continuous
  Permanent Improvement ......................... 217

**Chapter 22 Call to Action**............................. **221**
    How to Use This Call to Action List.................. 224
    Conclusion........................................ 225

*References* ............................................ *227*
*About the Author* ..................................... *229*
*Index*................................................. *231*

# List of Figures and Tables

| | | |
|---|---|---|
| Figure 1 | How one company evolved its business excellence road map from its business strategy. | 12 |
| Figure 2 | Example of business excellence road map evolved from business strategy. | 13 |
| Figure 3 | Example of excellence road map in a matrix format that defines long-term business objectives (*what*s) and strategies to achieve these objectives (*how*s). | 14 |
| Figure 4 | SIPOC versus COPIS. | 27 |
| Figure 5 | Strategic COPIS model. | 30 |
| Figure 6 | Strategic COPIS—detailed template with illustrations. | 31 |
| Figure 7 | Step-by-step guide on how to use the strategic COPIS template. | 36 |
| Figure 8 | Sample (partial) master list of business processes identified through strategic COPIS. | 40 |
| Figure 9 | Sample process map (first sheet—process overview). | 47 |
| Figure 10 | Sample process map (second sheet—process flowchart). | 48 |
| Figure 11 | Sample process map (third sheet—process details). | 49 |
| Figure 12 | Sample process map (fourth sheet—performance measures). | 50 |
| Figure 13 | "Layers" of performance measures. | 65 |
| Figure 14 | Sample 360-degree quality dashboard. | 69 |
| Table 1 | Data sources and recommended frequency for each layer of performance measurement. | 70 |
| Table 2 | 5S definitions. | 74 |

| Table 3 | DOWNTIMER: the nine types of muda or waste. | 80 |
| Figure 15 | Value stream mapping story. | 87 |
| Table 4 | The DMAIC problem-solving approach of Six Sigma. | 110 |
| Figure 16 | CEO's quality project review guidelines. | 112 |
| Figure 17 | CEO's quality project review template. | 113 |
| Figure 18 | Sample project charter (blank template). | 116 |
| Figure 19 | Example of root cause analysis through why–why or five whys technique. | 137 |
| Figure 20 | The cycle of root cause analysis. | 138 |
| Figure 21 | Matrix for identifying and prioritizing problems *before* they occur. | 150 |
| Figure 22 | Sample summary report of ideas generated and implemented. | 166 |
| Figure 23 | Sample detailed list of implemented ideas. | 166 |
| Figure 24 | The 360-degree knowledge management model. | 182 |
| Figure 25 | Sample business excellence model. | 190 |
| Figure 26 | The cycle of continuous permanent improvement. | 218 |
| Figure 27 | Strategic quality program implementation model. | 224 |

# Foreword

*Mikel J. Harry, PhD, the co-creator of Six Sigma, consultant to the world's top CEOs, and national best-selling author, is founder and CEO, Six Sigma Management Institute, Inc. He is also founder and CEO, The Great Discovery, LLC.*

It has been my distinct privilege to follow Arun Hariharan's career over the past decade. On several deeply meaningful occasions, we had the opportunity to interact and share our experiences and insights on the subject of business excellence. With each such encounter, it became more evident that his foundation of knowledge on the subject was growing exponentially in terms of both breadth and depth, not to mention taking on a sense of refinement and polish. At this point, I would have to say that Arun is a true master of business optimization. From this perspective, managers and executives alike should heed his wisdom and rely on his counsel.

Given these accolades, it is my professional opinion that his work is a "must read" for any leader who seeks to achieve their next level of business success. The author's direct and comprehensive hands-on experience and tactical command of business excellence are most evident as he covers all aspects of the quality domain—from strategy to implementation to results to the "people" aspects—in a logical flow. The author skillfully navigates the intersection of subject matter expertise and the "power of the pen." The book is smooth and highly readable. It takes hard work and a deep understanding of any subject to make it easy for others. This book reflects a level of insight and wisdom that only comes after the personal experience of many years of leading business excellence efforts. Full of relevant experiences, examples, and anecdotes, the book is like a knowledge warehouse that is packed full of what it takes to achieve success. The bottom line is simple. If you want to increase the velocity and quality of your business, I would strongly recommend reading this book.

Mikel J. Harry, PhD

# Foreword

*Dr. Kewal K. Nohria is the former chairman and managing director of Crompton Greaves Ltd., the former chairman of the Quality Promotion Board of India, and has held the office of president of industry associations like the Associated Chambers of Commerce and Industry of India (ASSOCHAM) and the Confederation of Indian Industry (CII).*

Arun Hariharan's book *Continuous Permanent Improvement* is a welcome addition to the literature of management. Most books so far have dealt with certain specific aspects of the journey to achieve excellence. This book synthesizes all the elements required to achieve business excellence, and could well be considered a reference book on the subject.

The author has not only dealt in depth with the theory of the subject, but has provided a practical road map to be followed while implementing a strategy to achieve business excellence. He has done this based on his actual hands-on experience in implementing excellence in a number of large companies.

I have personally witnessed the wonderful work done and the excellent results achieved by Arun at several companies during the last decade or so. I was very impressed by the depth, variety, and strategic linkage of quality initiatives in companies where Arun led the business excellence effort.

Arun rightly points out that excellence is a journey that never ends, but brings benefits at every step. It is not a one-time effort, but has to become a part of daily management. Therefore, top management commitment and visible involvement is a must. Arun further points out that any company can undertake this journey as long as there is a desire and determination to improve.

I think this book is a "must read" for business leaders, managers, teachers, and students who wish to learn about the theory, principles, and practice of business excellence.

Dr. Kewal K. Nohria

# Preface

On a recent visit to Japan, I had an opportunity to visit Toyota's headquarters. During a meeting with some of their top executives, I asked one of them what role the senior leadership played in Toyota's much admired quality philosophy. The reply I received was—like many things about Toyota and Japan—disarmingly simple, yet profound! He merely said, "We follow a philosophy of *improve every day.*"

That's it—*improve every day*! He had captured in three words the essence of what it takes to achieve, and sustain, excellence in business—or, for that matter, in any other field.

Just imagine the power of improvements, even small ones (in fact, *mostly* small ones), achieved every day, continuously over a period of weeks, months, years, decades! Needless to say, to be meaningful, any improvement, however small, needs to be permanent (*permanent* here means not rigid or "cast in stone," but sustainable for as long as it is relevant).

Companies like Toyota, and the leadership position in quality and business that they have been able to achieve, are living examples of the power of *improve every day*, or *continuous permanent improvement*.

And that is the theme of this book. The title *Continuous Permanent Improvement* seeks to convey the book's message.

*Continuous permanent improvement* (CPI) is not a new *ism*. The purpose of this book is not to expound any new theory or tools, but to share experiences in implementing existing methods with a bias toward business results. In fact, one of the important lessons we have learned is that most existing models or methods, if adhered to in the right spirit, will give results.

This book is a distillation of experiences and lessons learned from successes and mistakes in nearly three decades of experience, mostly working with business processes, systematic thinking, customer focus, quality, and performance measurements—for the collection of which I have used the broad name *business excellence*. In the last 28 years, I have had the opportunity to work with a variety of companies and industries as diverse as financial services, telecom, manufacturing, conglomerate, and management consulting. In addition, I have also been fortunate to interact with numerous business and quality leaders while speaking at conferences, at corporate management development programs, or at business schools.

During the last dozen years or so, I have had the opportunity to work with large companies such as Bharti Airtel and the Reliance Capital group.

Within the short span of a few years beginning around 1999, Bharti Airtel achieved tremendous year-on-year growth, becoming the industry leader in telecommunications in India, a position it has retained for many years at the time of this writing. The company started relatively small, but in less than 15 years grew to operate in about 20 countries and rank among the top five global mobile service providers in terms of number of customers.

The Reliance Capital group has several achievements to its credit. Most of the businesses in the group have achieved tremendous, rapid growth during the last several years. Some of its companies are among the leaders in their respective industries, and some are among the fastest to achieve profitability as compared to the competition. Recently, Nippon Life, one of the world's largest insurance companies, acquired a stake in two of Reliance Capital's group companies for a total of about INR 45 billion (approximately USD 830 million). This is the largest foreign direct investment ever in the Indian financial services industry up to the time of this writing.

Obviously, many factors have contributed to the achievements of these companies, including, but not limited to, visionary leadership, business acumen, human talent, execution capability, technology, investment in rapid growth in geographical presence and distribution networks, and so forth. Along with all of these, it is my firm conviction that their belief, strategy, and initiatives in business excellence also made a significant contribution to their business achievements (and their ability to sustain and build upon these achievements) over the years.

Two questions need to be asked and answered here. The first question is, have the companies in these examples reached perfection in business excellence? The second question is, has business excellence contributed to their achieving significant and sustained business results?

My answer to the first question (whether these companies—or any other company, for that matter—have reached perfection in business excellence) is *no*, I don't think so. Every company will continue to face challenges; what is important is to recognize problems and challenges as opportunities for continuous permanent improvement.

At the same time, my answer to the second question (has business excellence contributed to their business results) is a resounding *yes*. To repeat the cliché, quality is a journey, not a destination. The companies in these examples have shown that every step in this journey can give tremendous business results.

In fact, I believe it is good news if these companies, like any other company, have not reached perfection. This only makes them more *real*, and hence makes it easier for any company to aspire to get similar business results through business excellence. If only "perfect" companies could achieve this, many of us would not even start the journey.

So, the good news is, no, you don't have to be perfect, and, yes, every step in your business excellence journey can make your business stronger and give you results. After all, most businesses exist to achieve business results and not some so-called ideal of perfection.

In fact, my experience has been that having a business excellence road map and relentlessly implementing it started giving us quantifiable results within a few months, and continued giving results month after month, quarter after quarter, for years. More on the road map in Chapter 1.

While I have drawn on my nearly three decades of experience, this book is not about any specific companies or industries. Therefore, I believe the contents of this book can be applied in any industry— service or manufacturing or government or education or nonprofit. The target audience of this book is business, functional, and quality leaders. Business schools and students may also use it as a text or reference book for courses on business excellence or quality.

The book is intended to share the experience and results of organizations that have derived substantial and sustained business results by focusing on continuous permanent improvement. Its aim is to strengthen the belief of the reader in the strategic importance of CPI, because the stronger your belief, the bigger and more sustained will be your results. The book also covers challenges related to mindsets and other change management aspects that leaders typically will need to grapple with. Some of the very effective improvement methods and tools are explained in simple language with real examples, with senior business leaders in mind.

The book begins with the strategic aspects of business excellence and the role of the leadership. It talks about how to create a living road map for business excellence that is linked to the business strategy. This road map provides the broad framework that is essential for continuity and sustaining of business excellence efforts and results. The book goes on to talk about knowing who your customers are and how to listen to them. Next, it covers how to design processes and performance measures from the customer's perspective. These processes and measures are the basis or foundation for continuous permanent improvement. The book then covers how to improve performance and sustain the improvement. It talks about the role of both formal methods such as Lean, Six Sigma, and business excellence models, as well as ideas and innovation in continuous permanent improvement. It introduces the 360-degree knowledge management model, with examples of implementation and results. This is followed by a word to business leaders, quality professionals, and services. The cycle of continuous permanent improvement in the penultimate chapter provides a visual map or summary of the book's key message. The last chapter is a "call to action" that provides action steps on how to implement what is written in the book.

This book is not intended to be a detailed manual on specific tools and techniques. There are plenty of excellent training manuals available on the tools and techniques of Lean, Six Sigma, and other methodologies for the use of project leaders and teams that work on specific improvement projects. While there are numerous books on specific components of quality or business excellence, I felt there was a need for a book that puts it all together. I have tried to cover all aspects of excellence from strategy and culture to implementation and measurement, to results and sustaining those results—and attempted to put it in a logical flow. In other words, I have attempted to cover all components of a strategic quality program end to end (or "wing to wing" as some quality experts like to say). And I have made an effort to do so in simple, nontechnical language so that business leaders and senior executives from any business and any functional area find it easy to identify with and apply. This book tells the story of my actual experiences in implementing business excellence in various companies. The book mostly talks through examples and anecdotes; I thought that this way you would find it more interesting and, more importantly, easier to implement in your organization.

# 1

# Business or Excellence: Do We Have a Choice?

*Are you too busy for improvement? Look, you'll stop being busy either when you die or when the company goes bankrupt.*

—Shigeo Shingo

The company was a new entrant in its industry. Let's call it *company X* (you can think of your own company or some other company that you know). Quite a few established players had existed in the industry for several years before X came along. The current top three companies had each taken between seven and 10 years to reach their current size and position.

## AIMING FOR LEADERSHIP—FAST

X's ambition was to become the industry leader (in size) within its first three years of coming into being. They had capital available, and soon they were on an explosive growth path. In three years the number of cities in which the company rolled out its business grew by 10 times.

In the same period, the number of employees grew by 30 times! Almost all of these employees were salespeople. They were given tall targets and taller incentives if they met their targets. With extensive (and expensive) ad campaigns and aggressive (though not necessarily profitable) pricing to back them, many of the salespeople did initially succeed in selling to a number of customers.

## GROWING PAINS

With new customers being added in large numbers every day, the company was on a roll. Or, was it?

Within weeks, some customer complaints started trickling in. Several customers started complaining that they did not get what they were promised when they were promised, or that X's products and service were of inferior quality compared to the competition.

Some employees of company X (some of them recruited from competitors who were the current industry leaders) suggested that perhaps in the quest for rapid growth, the company had taken some shortcuts instead of creating a strong foundation at the back end, including robust processes, trained people, and tested technology. "Have we been too hasty in going out and selling before we create this infrastructure?" they wondered. "After all, our previous company took a few years to build this capability before they started to expand in a big way. And they would also think ahead to ensure that the infrastructure they built today was scalable to handle the size of the business a few years from now."

However, these were isolated voices, and they were soon shouted down by the high-testosterone sales types. "What wimps you are! Can't you see we're in the rapid growth phase? At this stage, we're building size and scale—and that's all that matters. Our target (and bonuses) depend on making this company number one in three years. Customer service, processes, and quality can wait. In the rapid growth phase, there will always be some complaints, but we can't let them get in the way of growth!"

## MAD ABOUT GROWTH

Unfortunately, the "rapid growth phase" turned out to be a "rapid money-burning phase." There was no institutionalization of standardized processes. The number of complaints was increasing, but the company turned a deaf ear to the voice of the customers. The leader of this business espoused a strategy of "crowding out" any complaining customers. "If 10 customers complain, go out and get another hundred customers. Then the complainers will be in the minority" was his message to his people.

When someone reminded him about the quality issues, he snapped back, "I'm sorry; I have a business to build and run. Quality can wait!"

The company seemed to have almost become mad in their pursuit of rapid growth. So mad that they almost forgot the reason for their existence—the customers. They actually started seeing customers—especially complaining customers—as a hurdle to realizing their growth dreams. The lowest point in this madness came one day when, confronted with increasing numbers of complaints, they shut down their customer service call center "to prevent the distracting voices from coming in." It was like cutting off the head to cure a headache!

## AN EXPENSIVE LESSON

In a few months, the company found itself hopelessly ill-equipped to serve the customers who had signed up (and there were a few hundred thousand of them). Many customers sent their complaints directly to the CEO or the chairman. Some even wrote to the industry regulator, and some to the media. Soon, the company was in the news for all the wrong reasons. Almost overnight, new customers stopped signing up. Existing customers started to leave.

Finally, the company realized its folly. They had gone out and started selling aggressively before they *had* anything to sell! Having learned the hard way that there are no shortcuts to success—especially with customers—they started doing what they should have done two years earlier: the back-end operations were strengthened with processes, trained people, and technology. They were sure now that the customers would start coming back.

But alas, it was too late. The company's image had taken such a beating that—as in the story of the boy who cried "wolf"—nobody believed them anymore. Neither promises of superior products and service nor cutting prices below the competition worked now. Customers just refused to come back!

That was seven years ago. Their "slow" competitors had taken about that much time to become industry leaders. And here was X, which had set out to topple the leaders in three years, still a nobody. They had sprinted fast, but got nowhere. The worst part was that their past actions had sealed their future, too; there seemed to be no chance of recovering now. Seven years and tons of money—wasted! Customer confidence—lost forever! They realized too late that *fast* can actually be *slow*.

The business leader, who had been in a hurry to set up the business first and worry about quality later, now realized that there *can* be no business without quality. After all, to have a business, you need customers, and to have customers, you need quality.

X had learned its lesson—that in any medium- to large-sized business, there is no substitute for building a foundation of standardized processes, trained people who will actually deliver what the salespeople promised to customers, and appropriate technology—*before* going out and selling and building scale. You can't scale up without processes!

The lesson for all of us from the sad story of X (I promise you some happy stories, too, as we go along) is that it is important, but not enough, to merely have a goal—in X's case the goal was to become the industry leader. It is equally important to have a plan or strategy on *how* to get there. X had no strategy, or, at best, an incomplete strategy. Their *how* was limited to throwing money at opening more offices and hiring more salespeople. However, they forgot a most important *how*—which is the need to plan for *excellence*. They saw excellence as something that would slow down their growth. In reality, however, it was running too fast without excellence that killed them. They finally realized that there can be no business without excellence.

> *It is important, but not enough, to merely have a goal . . . It is equally important to have a plan or strategy on how to get there.*

The next chapter is about business excellence strategy, or how to plan for excellence as part of your business strategy.

# 2
# Make Quality Your Strategy

*If you don't know where you are going, any road will take you there.*

—Cheshire Cat in *Alice's Adventures in Wonderland,* Lewis Carroll

Many readers have heard the old story of the blind men and the elephant. Six blind men were asked to stand around an elephant and identify the object or creature in front of them by touching and feeling it. The blind man who touched the tail thought that the elephant was a brush; the man who touched a leg thought it was a pillar; the one near its belly thought the elephant was a wall; and so forth. Each blind man tried to identify the elephant based on his limited perception, and none of them could see the whole elephant. True, the tail and trunk and legs are parts of the elephant, but the tail *is not* the elephant, neither is the trunk, nor any other part.

If you think about it, the story of quality in some organizations (not yours, I'm sure) is not very different. Too often, I have seen an ISO 9001 certification or a bunch of Six Sigma projects or some such initiative being seen as the "be all and end all" of quality in an organization. Of course, these are useful *components* of a quality program, but if some people think quality begins and ends with such initiatives, perhaps they are like the blind men in the story.

For a business leader, quality must be a *strategic tool* in achieving your business objectives in a sustained manner—objectives such as keeping your business profitable, keeping your customers from leaving you for the competition, and keeping your costs low—and doing all of these year after year. If you look at quality as your *strategy*, you are seeing the whole elephant.

> *For a business leader, quality must be a strategic tool in achieving your business objectives in a sustained manner—objectives such as keeping your business profitable, keeping your customers from leaving you for the competition, and keeping your costs low—and doing all of these year after year. If you look at quality as your strategy, you are seeing the whole elephant.*

This chapter tells the story of *how* the leaders of a large group of companies created a strategic quality road map that was linked with their business priorities.

## KNOW WHERE YOU WANT TO GO AND HOW TO GET THERE

Some years ago, I joined a large group of companies. At that time, most of the businesses in the group were relatively nascent. I was part of the leadership team that consisted of the CEOs of individual companies in the group, and group functional heads, such as myself. There were about 12 of us—we were called the Dirty Dozen!

One of the first things we did together as the leadership team was to sit and figure out the future of the group. Not the immediate future—as in next quarter—but the medium- to long-term future—five to 10 years ahead. There were two key questions: What were the objectives of the group and each of its businesses? And how do we get there?

The answer to the first question was relatively easy. Each company in the group wanted to be among the top three in its industry, by revenue, within five years. They wanted to achieve profitability faster than the competition. Creating value for shareholders through appreciation in the worth of their stock was another objective. In short, this group was targeting rapid growth and value unlocking.

The second question now was *how*? Clearly, there were several things that the group would need—capital, people, rapid expansion, distributors to sell their products, and so forth.

"But wait a minute," Dev, a member of the team, cautioned the rest, "each of our businesses is in a highly competitive industry. Let's remember that it's not enough to appoint distributors to sell our products, we need customers to *buy* them. And continue to buy. And tell their friends so that we get more customers and more business, to achieve the objectives we just discussed. Clearly, this is a challenge—probably the biggest challenge in front of us. We need to admit that our products are commodities—not significantly different from what the competition offers. Even if we differentiate our products by adding new features, or even introduce new products, competitors could copy them in no time. We also can not charge lower prices than competitors for too long without hurting ourselves because intense competition has already ensured that prices are quite competitive and margins are thin."

By this time, Dev was getting dirty looks from some of the others, but he continued unperturbed, "There's also another aspect we need to consider. That is the mind-boggling speed with which we want to grow. In two or three years, we want to achieve a size and scale that more established competitors have done in seven or eight years. I know of companies that have tried to do this, and only succeeded in creating utter chaos and customer complaints."

Some of Dev's colleagues could hold back no longer. "What are you getting at, young man? Are you trying to discourage us? Haven't you heard of BHAG (big hairy audacious goals)?"

"Sorry, I didn't mean to sound negative," Dev hastened to reply, "I am as eager as anybody else in this room for us to achieve the goals we have set for our group. The questions I threw out were only meant to provoke all of us to think *how* we can actually increase our chances of achieving our BHAG."

Baird, the group president, who headed the leadership team, now spoke. "I think young Dev has a point. Don't we all know of companies, hopefully not ours, that set out to achieve very ambitious sales targets in a short time but didn't create the required capability to meet their promises to customers? I can think of quite a few cases where a company, in the quest for rapid growth, only succeeded in getting itself into a big mess from which it never recovered. Obviously, it's not going to be enough to go out there and make promises to customers, we need to be able to fulfill our promises. More importantly, we need to be able to fulfill our promises consistently." The president continued, "However, given the ethos of our group, I don't think anybody, not even Dev, is suggesting that we water down our targets or slow down. One point being made here is that it is important to have a goal, or a BHAG as in our case, so that we know where we want to go. The other, equally important point is to know *how* to get there."

Eventually, the others came around to seeing the point. The discussion now turned to the *how* part. The more obvious part of this *how* was resources—money, people, geographic expansion, and so forth, to fuel the rapid growth. But as the discussion progressed and each member of the leadership team started sharing their experiences and giving their inputs, it became more and more obvious that they were going to need something more than money, employees, and other resources.

They were going to need a scaffolding that they could use to climb up toward the goal, a broad road map or framework that would guide them to the target.

To give an idea of how rapidly the group was planning to scale up, one business planned to go from 10 offices to 200 offices across the country and from 90 employees to 5000 employees—all of this in the next year! One leader said, "The only way we're going to be able to scale up so rapidly—and do it smoothly—is to have standardized ways of working. If I have four offices and 20 employees today, and plan to grow to 20 offices and 100 employees in three months, the only way I can achieve this is to document *how the work is done* and use this to train the new people. If we want them to start delivering from day one, we need to be able to tell them, 'here's how we work, now go out there and do it.'" In other words, *standardized processes*.

Dev looked relieved. *Now* the discussion was going somewhere. He threw out another question, "Shouldn't we also have a way of knowing how well—or not so well—we're progressing toward our goal?"

Someone answered immediately, "That's easy. We have our sales and revenue targets. If we achieve them each quarter, we know we are on the right track. If we don't, we're not."

"That's like saying that if the patient dies, we know that the treatment didn't work. But isn't there something that could tell us a little in advance—like an early warning signal—so that we can do something if we sense we are going off course?" It was the president who spoke.

A suggestion came—"If customers don't like our products or service, they will complain. We could measure the number of complaints. If there are no complaints, we know we're doing well." Another person said, "We could also do an annual customer satisfaction survey."

Dev said, "Good suggestions. It is important to measure complaints or have other ways of knowing what customers think about us. But again, is that enough? Remember, by the time a customer complains, they are already unhappy with us. Is there some way of knowing about problems *before* the problem reaches the customer—so that we can *prevent* it? Besides, not every unhappy customer complains. In fact, research shows that only a minority of unhappy customers takes the trouble to complain. Most of them just take their business elsewhere."

Another team member chipped in, "That reminds me, the company I used to work for earlier had what they called 'process measures' that helped them to identify problems *before* the problem reached the customer. It was an automobile manufacturer, and they used to measure how many, if any, defective parts were made in each of the lines in their plant. They also measured defects in inputs coming from suppliers. This way, they were able to detect problems and prevent them from reaching the customer. Although that was in a manufacturing company, I guess we could have process measures in any type of industry that has processes, including our own."

Baird looked pleased. "I am glad you are planning to have measurements that will give us signals about our performance early enough when we have relatively more control and could actually do something about it. After all, we can manage and improve what we can measure. To continue with the automobile example, if a problem of defective parts supplied by one particular supplier is detected even before the defective part is used to manufacture a car, it's easier to solve the problem either by getting the supplier to fix the problem at their end or moving to a defect-free supplier. It's much more difficult to try and win back customers *after* they encounter faulty vehicles. In fact, it's almost impossible to prevent the loss of customers and revenue that is likely to result if we wait until the problem reaches the customer."

The discussion continued late into the evening. Most of the discussion now was on topics like business processes, systematic thinking, customer focus, quality, performance measurements, and so forth. I have used the broad name *business excellence* for these.

The group agreed that once they had defined *what* they were out to achieve, it was equally important to define *how*. And along with the usual *how*s such as capital and people (resources), business excellence was clearly an important means to achieving the goal.

The group then went on to define a business excellence strategy, or road map, that was aligned with its business strategy. The road map provided a guideline as to how the group would sequence its business excellence initiatives, such as designing business processes, laying down measurements, and establishing methods for performance improvement. The road map was a broad framework for the group's business excellence initiatives, thus ensuring continuity. It helped the businesses improve their performance continuously and in a sustained manner.

At the same time, the road map provided the flexibility to align initiatives with business priorities in any particular year, while still providing a broad framework for continuity and building upon previous efforts and results. For example, during a particularly severe global economic downturn, the group decided that the most sensible business strategy for that year would be to protect profitability by cost control and eliminating waste—rather than trying to grow revenues. During that year, most improvement projects were aimed at identifying and eliminating waste, and streamlining processes to make them lean. That year, the business excellence projects were the biggest contributor to profitability.

Several years down the line, how did the group do in achieving the BHAG that it had set for itself? Not too badly. Most of its businesses are among the revenue leaders in their respective industries. They are all profitable, and some of them were among the fastest in their industry to achieve break-even and become profitable. And value creation for shareholders has happened in a big way.

While the example of one group is given in this chapter, I have personally experienced this firsthand in several companies and groups over the years. And I am sure many readers have seen similar examples, too.

## DO YOU HAVE A BUSINESS EXCELLENCE ROAD MAP?

This chapter is not about any particular company or industry. It is about the importance of having a strategy, or road map, for business excellence (or *quality* or any other name that your company may use) that provides a broad guiding framework to ensure continuity, and at the same time is flexible enough to meet current business priorities. Even more important is for this business excellence strategy to flow from, or be aligned with, the overall medium- to long-term business strategy. An example of how one company evolved its business excellence strategy from its business strategy is shown in Figure 1. It is most important to never lose sight of the road map, but relentlessly follow and implement it.

While the example in this chapter spoke about a group of nascent businesses, it is important and beneficial for every business, at whatever stage in its life cycle, to have a business excellence road map and implement it.

Two sample business excellence road maps are shown in Figures 2 and 3. These are shown as examples only. The same road map may not work for every company. What is important is for your organization to have *your own* road map for business excellence aligned with your business strategy, and then relentlessly implement the road map. The best people to create this road map for each organization are its own business leaders.

Also, even for one company, the road map, once created, is not unchangeable. Unforeseen or drastic changes in the internal or external environment of the organization may necessitate revisiting the road map. In fact, in such situations it is better to realign the road map so that it can continue to contribute to the organization achieving its business goals in the new environment.

That said, however, it is essential to remember that the road map is meant to be a broad framework or guideline. It is important to keep it that way, and not make it a narrow "plan for the year" or a to-do list. We have learned from experience that it is best to think ahead about your vision for your business at least five to 10 years into the future, and then design the business excellence road map that will help you achieve your vision. We kept it that way in several businesses that I had an opportunity to work with over many

| |
|---|
| **Short-term goal: Attain market leadership in each line of business**<br>*How?* Through rapid expansion.<br>Robust, standardized business processes are a must for smooth and rapid scaling up<br>***Therefore, business excellence road map part 1 is: business process excellence*** |
| **Long-term goal: Maintain and increase competitive edge**<br>*How?* Through:<br>1. Continuous performance improvements<br>2. Organizational culture of quality, customer orientation, data- and analysis-based working<br>3. Breakthrough performance improvements<br>4. Consistent customer experience through elimination of variation<br>5. Maximizing productivity and internal efficiencies<br>***Therefore, business excellence road map part 2 is: continuous improvement*** |
| **Long-term goal: Further widen competitive edge through speed in business results**<br>*How?* Through organization-wide culture of sharing and replication of knowledge, and elimination of reinvention<br>***Therefore, business excellence road map part 3 is: knowledge management*** |

**Figure 1**  How one company evolved its business excellence road map from its business strategy.

years. We never found a need to tinker with the road map from year to year. In fact, the business excellence road map lent solidity and continuity to the business excellence initiatives, and, in fact, to the business itself. The road map helped the businesses to steadily build upon their strengths and successes year after year, continuously learn from mistakes, and improve. And, most importantly, ensure that the improvements were *permanent*.

I like to think of the road map as a large, slow but sure outer wheel, and specific initiatives or projects within the framework of

> **Part 1 Foundation—business process excellence**
> - Identify business processes and performance measures
> - Design and implement standardized processes
> - Measure implementation through process compliance audits
> - Put in place quality- and customer-related performance measures (dashboards)
> - Begin measurement of customer voice (customer satisfaction surveys, complaints)
> - ISO 9001 or other process certification
>
> **Part 2—Continuous improvement**
> - Institutionalize system for root cause analysis and continuous process improvement
> - Analyze and review quality and customer measures (dashboards)
> - Quality improvement projects/Lean Six Sigma
> - Closure of nonconformities identified in ISO 9001 or other process audits
> - Process simplification/streamlining/refinements through kaizen and 5S
>
> **Part 3—Knowledge management**
> - Promote synergy, sharing, and replication of internal and external best practices
> - Promote generation and implementation of innovative ideas—create a "process for innovation"
> - Create communities of experts and knowledge bases
>
> Note: The initial creation of standardized processes and measurements as described in part 1 above would precede parts 2 and 3. After this, the three parts are not sequential, but continuous, never-ending, and work in tandem to take the organization to higher levels of business excellence.

**Figure 2**  Example of business excellence road map evolved from business strategy.

the road map as smaller, faster inner wheels. The "inner wheels" give quick results, while at the same time, being part of the larger framework of the outer wheel, they work toward a larger common direction and unified purpose.

## 14 Chapter Two

| Objectives (What) \ Strategies (How) | Deliver clearly superior service | Expansion of service by way of acquisitions | Deploy innovative products and services | Outsource non-core activities | Develop leadership pool | Focus on corporate segment | Good corporate governance practices | Continuous improvement projects | Knowledge management | Measure | Actual 20x1 | Target 20xx |
|---|---|---|---|---|---|---|---|---|---|---|---|---|
| To be the leader in customer services by 20xx | | | | | | | | | | Customer satisfaction scores | | |
| To be the leader in revenue market share by 20xx | | | | | | | | | | Revenue share | | |
| To be among the top 10 brands by 20xx | | | | | | | | | | Leading surveys | | |
| To be among the top 10 employers by 20xx | | | | | | | | | | Leading surveys | | |
| To continue to be among the top 10 companies in market capitalization | | | | | | | | | | Market capitalization | | |

**Figure 3** Example of business excellence road map in a matrix format that defines long-term business objectives (*whats*) and strategies to achieve these objectives (*hows*).

> *I like to think of the road map as a large, slow but sure outer wheel, and specific initiatives or projects within the framework of the road map as smaller, faster inner wheels. The "inner wheels" give quick results, while at the same time, being part of the larger framework of the outer wheel, they work toward a larger common direction and unified purpose.*

In the next chapter, we will look at whose job business excellence is—particularly the role of the leadership.

# 3
# Whose Job Is Excellence?

> *Quality is too important to be left to the quality department.*
>
> —Philip Crosby

This chapter seeks to highlight an important aspect of leadership and corporate governance that deserves much more focus in most organizations than it receives today.

Before you read on, close your eyes and take one minute to make a mental list of companies worldwide that are renowned for sustained financial performance and value creation for shareholders (as compared to their competitors) by making business excellence their key strategic weapon to achieve this (*business excellence* here means the combination of product/service quality, customer focus, productivity, cost/waste consciousness, and continuous improvement).

How many companies do you have on your list? Chances are you have some great examples, but most likely it's a small list. The question we now need to ask ourselves is, why don't we have more names on this list? Given the huge number of companies in every industry that haven't made it onto your list, isn't this a great opportunity for sustained financial performance just waiting to be tapped across industries all over the world?

Why isn't the list longer than what you came up with? Perhaps you missed a few, given the one-minute constraint. But I believe that a good part of the blame for your list not being longer lies with the board of directors and the CEO. This chapter looks at the role of the board and the CEO in helping companies achieve superior and sustained performance by making business excellence a key strategic weapon.

## DO BOARDS REPRESENT CUSTOMERS ENOUGH?

Do boards in companies that you know of do a good job of representing the customer as a key stakeholder (we're talking of the customer who pays for the company's product or service)?

In most companies, quality of products and service as experienced by customers is a key differentiator from competition. In that case, shouldn't quality be a board meeting topic? Unless one is only interested in the very short term, customer satisfaction is a key determinant of sustained financial results and shareholder value.

In today's world the average CEO tenure is getting shorter. This could be one reason very few CEOs look beyond short-term financial outcomes. While there are notable exceptions, many CEOs have no clear thoughts on institution building or on sustaining the financial outcomes beyond the short term.

Many CEOs never get questioned on anything beyond their results for the last quarter or their plans for the next quarter or, at best, the next year. Some CEOs are required to present their plan for the next one or more years, but these presentations rarely go beyond guesstimates of sales and profit numbers.

The first thing that needs to happen for this to change is for the board to start asking some new questions at board meetings that they have never asked before.

## QUESTIONS THAT THE BOARD MUST ASK

Do boards in companies that you know of ask their CEOs about the following:

- What are our customers saying? . . . about our company? . . . about the competition?
- How many customer complaints did we get last month or quarter?
- What are the most frequent complaints?
- What percentage of these complaints were resolved within our target time?
- What improvement actions were done as part of the process to *prevent* such defects?

- Show examples of continuous, permanent improvements during the last quarter.
- Show examples of identification and elimination of waste.
- Show examples of productivity improvement or cost reduction.

## HOW TO ENSURE THAT THE BOARD DOESN'T GET INTO TOO MUCH DETAIL

Some may argue that these questions are too "tactical" or "operational" and that boards should focus on more "strategic" matters. However, the truth is that these questions are well worth the board's time. If business excellence is a key determinant of your company's competitive success, sustained financial performance, and shareholder value creation, it most certainly is the business of the board. Obviously, the involvement of the board can be kept at a reasonably high level, while ensuring that the CEO and senior executives in their teams go into more detail.

In addition to spending some time discussing these questions at the board meetings, companies could have a "quality committee" similar to other (often statutory) committees for audit, investment, and risk management. The quality committee could be headed by one of the directors on the board.

## WHY CAN'T ONE DIRECTOR REPRESENT THE CUSTOMER AS A KEY STAKEHOLDER?

While, on paper, boards are expected to represent the interests of various stakeholders, in practice, most boards end up only representing the interests of the larger shareholders. If a company has several directors on the board, do they all need to be the same kind of people asking the same kind of financial and regulatory questions? No doubt, financial and compliance aspects are important, and boards must govern these. However, the question here is, why can't a couple of directors focus on these aspects, while at least one director makes it their business to represent the interests of the customers who pay for the company's products?

# WHY THE BOARD MUST ASK THESE QUESTIONS

Whose job is business excellence? The answer is "everybody's," but it has to begin at the top. These "questions that the board must ask" above *must* start at the board because if the board does not ask these questions, CEOs will not ask these questions . . . and if CEOs do not ask these questions, *nobody* in the organization will ask these questions.

While this may seem like common sense, the ground reality is that many CEOs today have a short-term agenda because they are seldom, if at all, questioned about institution building. This short-term focus could actually prove to be harmful to the interests of customers (and hence, eventually, the business and shareholders).

Board members, including independent directors, must start asking quality- and customer-related questions at board meetings, and ask them regularly and repeatedly.

If boards do not ask these questions, there will be no quality . . . without quality, there will be no customers . . . and without customers, there will be no business. And competitors whose boards *do* ask these questions will walk away with your customers and your business.

> *If boards do not ask these questions, there will be no quality . . . without quality, there will be no customers . . . and without customers, there will be no business.*

# INDICATORS OF ORGANIZATIONS WHERE THE BOARD FOCUSES ON QUALITY AND CUSTOMERS

The following are some indicators of organizations with progressive boards that focus on business excellence and customers:

- Business excellence is an agenda item at board meetings.
- Quality- and customer-related measures form part of the CEO's performance evaluation.

- The board encourages thinking about and measuring performance from the customer's perspective.
- There exists a distinct and dedicated team focused on continuous improvement and quality on the ground for customers. This team is empowered and encouraged to act as the "representative of the customer."
- A senior management person holds responsibility for business excellence and continuous improvement.

## THE CEO'S ROLE

Without exception, companies worldwide that have gotten significant results from business excellence have one thing in common: excellence is among the top items on the CEO's agenda and on the CEO's *mind*. Remember, it needs to be top priority on the CEO's *personal* agenda, and this can not be delegated.

> *Companies worldwide that have gotten significant results from business excellence have one thing in common: excellence is among the top items on the CEO's agenda and on the CEO's mind.*

Another thing common in successful companies is that the CEO's agenda tends to be a rather small list. If the company has too many strategic initiatives, it is unlikely to be able to focus on any of them. They will eat up precious management and employee time all the same because each initiative on the list must have its share of committees and brainstorming sessions and meetings. Delivering results is another matter altogether.

Effective business leaders never let their companies lose focus on the real business imperatives—and have a small number of critical initiatives as part of their strategy to achieve these imperatives. These few initiatives then get complete attention and focus. So, if you are the CEO, make sure your agenda is a small list and business excellence figures high on your list.

Also, CEOs need to ensure that their senior executives (typically, people directly reporting to the CEO) are accountable for implementation of the business excellence road map and initiatives. Excellence-related measures must form a significant part of the CEO's own and their senior executives' performance appraisals.

Some years ago, a friend who works with a large bank complained, "My CEO always wants a 'helicopter' view and starts yawning the moment I go into any detail." If you are the CEO, do you ask for a "30,000-foot" or "high-level" view of things? I have known a few CEOs who would only want to be involved at a "strategic" level and would disengage the moment we got into territory they considered "operational."

My friend's bank started its business excellence program a few years ago. Around the same time, a large telecommunications company also started its business excellence program. It so happened that both the bank and the telecom company engaged the same consultant and followed the same methodology in their business excellence implementation.

Two years later, the telecom company's business excellence strategy was showing significant business results and improved customer satisfaction. In the bank, nothing much had changed, except that they had created an army of people who had attended training programs.

The only difference between the two companies was that the telecom company's CEO had been spending time every month reviewing the progress of the business excellence program, while the bank's CEO was sent a "high-level" business report each month, which occasionally included one line on excellence.

For most companies that have achieved sustained competitive success, business excellence is a key strategic tool. For the telecom company in the example, business excellence was a strategic weapon—and hence worth the CEO's time.

The days of the "30,000-foot" or "helicopter" CEO are over. Today CEOs need to go into some detail personally. Today's world is too competitive, and successful CEOs today are more hands-on and more willing to go into details. Remember, business excellence is the CEO's job.

## CHICKEN AND EGG

Is it worth the leadership's time? My experience time and again is that the leadership gets the results that it *expects* from business excellence (I believe that's true for other strategic initiatives as well). I have lost count of the number of times I have come across a company or its leadership failing to achieve any significant or sustained results because they never *expected* significant results to begin with! On the other hand, I have also seen companies that achieved substantial, quantifiable, and sustained results from excellence simply because that's what the business leader expected. (I have had the opportunity to work with a few myself—and what a pleasure it has been!)

> **Leadership gets the results that it expects *from* business excellence.**

It works like chicken-and-egg in a positive sense. The leadership expects more, and hence gets more involved, and hence gets more results, and hence finds it worth their time, and sets their expectations even higher . . . and the cycle repeats.

## EXCELLENCE IS EVERYONE'S JOB

Starting with the board and CEO, business excellence is the job of everyone in the organization. Everyone, irrespective of seniority or functional role, needs to do their jobs right the first time, meet their customer's requirement, and figure out ways to continuously improve their performance. And everyone has customers—it's just that some of them may be internal customers.

If the organization has a business excellence road map, and if implementing this road map is a primary agenda item for the CEO and senior leaders, it helps to align the efforts of people down the line with the organizational road map. While everyone continues to do their own job and play their role in the business, they now also need to do their job *well* to contribute toward excellence.

## IS QUALITY THE JOB OF THE "QUALITY DEPARTMENT"?

Quality is too important to be left to, well, people like me! Business excellence is not a bunch of "quality people" sitting in a corner of your company doing projects. Excellence is the job of everyone in the company. Your business excellence program needs to be a mass movement involving every one of your people.

Your quality department alone can not make your company's business excellence strategy a success. However, having a few crazy people who are obsessed with customers and passionate about your company's business excellence road map and its success can certainly be a huge catalyst.

> *Your quality department alone can not make your company's business excellence strategy a success. However, having a few crazy people who are obsessed with customers and passionate about your company's business excellence road map and its success can certainly be a huge catalyst.*

In short, the substance of this chapter is that business excellence is the responsibility of everyone in the organization, beginning with the leadership. Involvement of the board and the CEO will help to ensure that your company's business excellence initiatives address your strategic business priorities and galvanize the efforts of everyone in the organization toward this. And having a bunch of crazy catalysts who will infect the rest of the organization with their enthusiasm for business excellence does help.

In the next chapter, we will look at where to begin your business excellence journey. Of course, creating your business excellence road map was a beginning. But in the next chapter, we will actually get off the drawing board and get our hands and feet dirty by landing on the ground and stepping into the shoes of—who else but your customer!

# 4
# Begin from the Beginning: Know Who Your Customers Are and What They Want

> *Quality is not what the supplier puts in. It is what the customer gets out and is willing to pay for.*
>
> —Peter F. Drucker

Years ago, I invited a Six Sigma expert to speak to the leadership team of the company I worked for. One of the things that he told us was that "the fastest way to reach Six Sigma is—well—to cut out the customer"! He narrated examples of companies that had tried to make their performance look good by defining their performance measures in an inward-looking way rather than from the customer's point of view—and the eventual sad end that they (the company, not the customers) met. He was cautioning us against falling into this trap of making our internal measures look good while ignoring the customer's viewpoint. And I couldn't agree with him more.

---

***The fastest way to reach Six Sigma is—well—to cut out the customer.***

---

I had the opportunity to introduce and participate in the implementation of a concept that I call *strategic COPIS* (explained in detail in this chapter) at eight large businesses—very different from one another—over an eight-year period. This is possibly the first such organization-wide strategic application of the COPIS approach. The application of strategic COPIS has contributed to significant and sustained business benefits over the years. This chapter introduces the concept of strategic COPIS and shares the experience of applying it in real businesses. Through firsthand experiences and examples, I have tried to explain the concept in a manner that makes it easy for senior managers in any industry to understand and apply it in their own business.

In several businesses that I worked with, the first step in the business excellence road map was to put in place their business processes and performance measures. Most business, government, and even not-for-profit organizations have processes. Generally, processes are documented. Most organizations also have performance measurements. But step back for a moment and ask two fundamental but strategic questions: "What business processes do we need in the first place?" and "What should we measure?" This chapter is about finding the answers to these questions with the help of strategic COPIS.

But wait a minute—even before asking the two questions mentioned above, it may be a good idea (as we learned from experience) to go back another step and ask an even more fundamental question: "*Who* is your customer, in the first place?" This sounds simple enough, but believe me when I say that "customer" had different meanings to different people from the same leadership team of the same company—and I have seen this in company after company. So, the first step is to know who your customer is. We're not talking here about some "know your customer" or KYC exercise that companies sometimes do—often pushed by regulators (at times, KYC turns out to be more of "harass your customer," and I often wonder if it should be renamed as HYC, but I digress . . . .). All that is meant here by *customer* is the person who *pays* for your product or service.

Having identified who our *paying* customer was, the next question was "What does the customer want?" We realized that all we needed to do to find this out was to go and *ask* the customer! In businesses with huge numbers of customers (some of our businesses had more than a million customers), we did a bit of role-play. We got people inside the company (such as the CEO and their leadership team) to *pretend* for a while that they were the customer of their business and guess what they would want from the company if *they* were the customer. Easier said than done, fun, uncomfortable at times, but unforgettable—more on that story later in the chapter. Of course, we didn't blindly believe our guesses on what customers wanted. We actually went out and checked with some *real* customers, and had a few surprises as well. These companies used this knowledge of what customers wanted to determine *what the company would do* (products and service) and *how* (processes).

## SIPOC AND COPIS

The concept of SIPOC (an acronym for supplier–input–process–output–customer) is fairly common among business process experts as a logical way of looking at a process as a series of steps that convert an input (for example, steel) into an output (for example, a car). Inputs come from suppliers, and the outputs go to customers.

The opposite idea of COPIS (customer–output–process–input–supplier, see Figure 4) has also been around for some time, particularly used in Six Sigma quality projects as an "outside-in" approach to looking at and possibly streamlining a business process from the customer's point of view. Such an application of the COPIS concept as a tool can be described as *operational COPIS*. It is limited to the scope of an individual project—usually a single process or, at best, a few more processes that impact that process.

## COPIS AS A STRATEGY

The idea of *strategic* COPIS took root in my mind more than a decade ago. I used to see operational COPIS being used as a tool in Six Sigma projects, and think to myself, "Aha! Why can't we do this for the whole company?" That opportunity came a couple of years later. Experience has shown that businesses can derive much broader and more sustained benefits through strategic COPIS, that is, applying the COPIS concept at a strategic or organization-wide scale, and

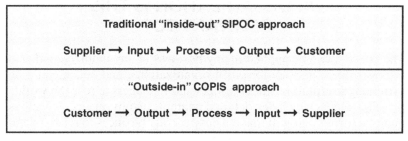

**Figure 4** SIPOC versus COPIS.

not limiting it to an individual process or project. What follows is the story of application of strategic COPIS at a number of businesses. The COPIS approach has been used at a companywide level to identify *who* a business's customers are in the first place and what business processes and performance measures the business needs.

The organization-wide application of COPIS has provided answers to the questions "what business processes to have" and "what to measure." The experience of having applied strategic COPIS and having used its outputs (that is, the business processes and performance measures identified through COPIS) for several years has shown that the strategic COPIS application gave the businesses a solid foundation for continuous improvement in the form of *relevant* business processes and performance measures. This has been the basis for all improvement ever since. It has also been a key pillar for sustaining of improvements and business performance year after year. It can now be said through hindsight that we would have had no foundation for continuous improvement (or, at best, a rather shaky one) if we had not applied strategic COPIS first and used its output to put basic business processes and performance measures in place.

> *It can now be said through hindsight that we would have had no foundation for continuous improvement (or, at best, a rather shaky one) if we had not applied strategic COPIS first and used its output to put basic business processes and performance measures in place.*

## WHAT TYPE OF BUSINESS OR ORGANIZATION IS THIS RELEVANT TO?

The concept can be applied in any business in any industry, and also in government and not-for-profit organizations, and hence could be extremely useful to business leaders and managers across the world.

This chapter includes detailed examples from service as well as manufacturing that will make it easy for any business to relate to and apply COPIS in their own business.

## THE STORY OF HOW STRATEGIC COPIS WAS APPLIED

The detailed, outside-in, step-by-step strategic COPIS model (see Figure 5) will make the concept clear. Figure 6 shows extended, detailed examples (one continuous story from service and one from manufacturing) that will enable managers from any business to understand the concept and apply it in their own business.

During the last several years, I had the opportunity to facilitate the application of strategic COPIS at eight different large businesses—in most cases right from the inception of the business. The experiment has proved to be highly beneficial to the businesses, with the strategic COPIS application's output actually forming the basis of identifying and putting in place business processes and performance measures.

Here's what we did, step by step: The first step was a facilitated workshop at each business, with the business head (CEO) and senior leaders of that business. We especially made sure that senior managers leading areas that impact customers participated. During the workshop, we all put ourselves in the customer's shoes and pretended that we were the customer (as I said earlier, this was easier said than done, and some of us kept going back to wearing our old "hats" but were gently pulled back into the customer's shoes by the workshop facilitator). We later realized that "wearing the customer's hat" is perhaps the most important part of the whole exercise, not to mention that it was a valuable—though at times uncomfortable—learning experience for many of us.

> *"Wearing the customer's hat" is perhaps the most important part of the whole exercise, not to mention that it was a valuable—though at times uncomfortable—learning experience for many of us.*

We started by first agreeing (after some debate) that the business exists for its customers—or, at least, that the business depends on customers for its existence.

Now take a look at the COPIS template in Figures 5 and 6. We completed, as a team, the first column of the template "Customer

## Customer requirements

| Customer experience points | Output required by customer | Voice of customer/customer satisfaction (CSAT) measure(s) | Data source for measure | Frequency of measurement | "Verbatim" feedback/customer voice related to this process |
|---|---|---|---|---|---|
| | | | | | |

## Customer satisfaction

## Internal measures

| Related internal measure(s) | Definition of "defect" | Data source for defect | Definition of "Opportunity for defect" | Data source for "Opportunity for defect" | Sigma level | Frequency of internal measurement | Process(es) that will deliver these output(s) | Process owner |
|---|---|---|---|---|---|---|---|---|
| | | | | | | | | |

## Process

## Suppliers

| Inputs required from other functions/departments | Internal and external supplier(s) (Cross-functional dependencies) | In-process or input measure(s) (Internal service-level agreements required) | Audit checkpoint(s) | Opportunities for customer delight | Opportunities for differentiation against competition |
|---|---|---|---|---|---|
| | | | | | |

## Inputs → Audit → Competitive edge

☐ Zone 1 represents voice of customers and measures related to product or service quality as experienced by customers
▨ Zone 2 represents voice of the process and internal/process quality related measures
▨ Zone 3 represents opportunities for delivering superior quality that exceeds customer expectations

**Figure 5** Strategic COPIS model.

Begin from the Beginning: Know Who Your Customers Are   31

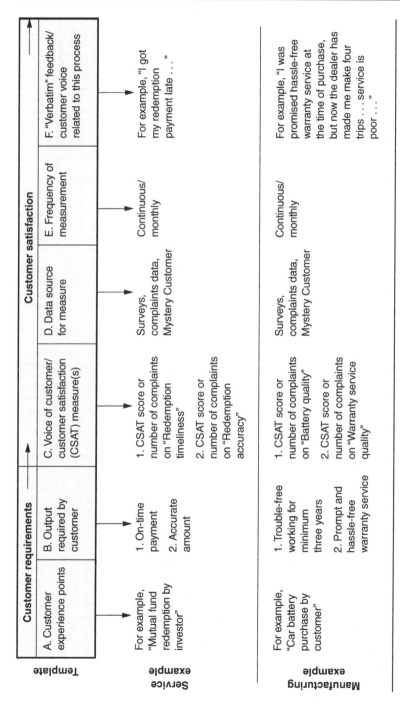

Figure 6a   Strategic COPIS—detailed template with illustrations.

## 32 Chapter Four

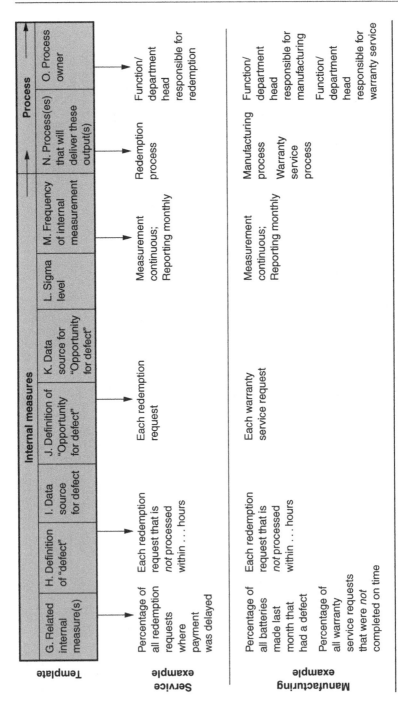

**Figure 6b** Strategic COPIS—detailed template with illustrations.

# Begin from the Beginning: Know Who Your Customers Are

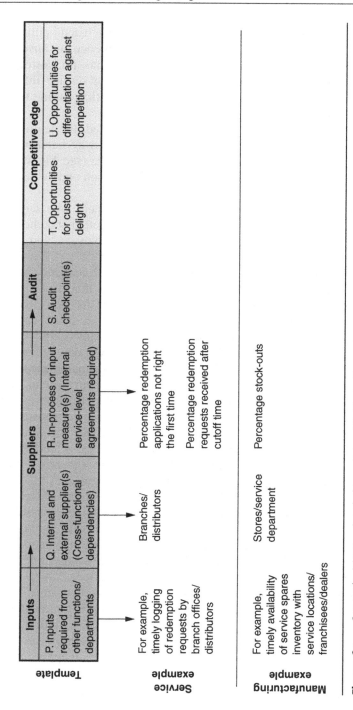

**Figure 6c** Strategic COPIS—detailed template with illustrations.

experience points" (see column A in Figure 6a). We listed in this column all key "touch points" where customers experience our business, its products, or services. Typical experience points for customers could be the initial purchase experience, ongoing service interactions, contacting customer service, visiting our office, online transactions, and so on.

Once all common experience points were listed, the team took one experience point at a time and went all the way horizontally to the right of the template, one column at a time (see Figures 6a through 6c). The facilitator moderated the discussion and helped fill in the template for each experience point.

Once the exercise was completed for customers who *buy* the company's products or service, it was repeated for other stakeholders such as distributors, shareholders, regulators, employees, and other internal customers.

At the end of the strategic COPIS workshop, we realized that we had created a complete "master list" of processes that the business needs to have and performance measures related to each process. At the end of the COPIS exercise, column N in Figure 6b becomes the master list of business processes that your company needs. All the other columns in Figures 6a through 6c will give you details for each process, such as who owns the process, what performance measures the process needs, and so forth. Performance measures are at three levels—voice of the customer, process-related output measures, and in-process measures. Several examples of performance measures at each level are shown in Figures 6a through 6c. Indeed, the strategic COPIS output sheet *was* the map of the entire business—it contained everything that needed to happen in the company, who was responsible for each process, and how to measure performance.

Before proceeding further, we validated the outputs or findings of the workshop with some real customers. This helped ensure that what we *thought* important for customers was actually so. We did have a couple of surprises when we spoke to actual customers, and the necessary corrections on the COPIS output were made.

We now had the answers to two strategic questions: "What business processes do we need?" and "What should we measure?" This was followed by detailed documentation and mapping, and implementation on the ground of the processes thus identified. Actual adherence to each process is measured through periodic process-compliance audits. We will read the story of process mapping in the next chapter.

Next, the business put in place the measurements identified through COPIS. The CEO and their leadership team meet monthly for a "dashboard review" to monitor the actual performance trends on these measures. This dashboard review at each business has happened every month, without missing a month, for years now.

At each business, the COPIS workshop generated a large number of performance measures. With the help of each CEO, we identified the top-priority (vital few) measures that the CEO will personally review and the more-detailed measures pertaining to each process that must be monitored and reviewed by the respective process owners. Chapter 6 tells the story of performance measurement in detail.

A step-by-step guide on how to use the strategic COPIS template is given in Figure 7.

## KEEPING PROCESSES AND PERFORMANCE MEASURES CURRENT

The master list of processes and performance measures is revisited at least once a year to keep it relevant and current. Minor changes such as adding or deleting a process or measure may be required from time to time with changes in the business environment.

For large-scale changes that may be necessitated by radical changes in the business model, market scenario, competitive environment, or other factors, it may be beneficial to go through the strategic COPIS workshop again to identify processes and performance measures relevant in the new environment. This is a judgment call to be taken by the business leaders depending on the scale of change.

In any event, it may be a good idea to repeat the strategic COPIS workshop about once every two or three years. It would help validate the existing master list of processes and performance measures and bring fresh ideas. The experience would also keep the customer-centric culture alive.

## IS IT RELEVANT ONLY IN A NEW BUSINESS?

I have been involved in both new businesses and relatively older businesses that have existed for several years, and my experience was that strategic COPIS can be applied with significant business benefit by

1. The application of strategic COPIS is best done through a facilitated workshop attended by the business head (CEO) and senior leaders of a business. Senior managers leading areas that impact customers must definitely participate. During the workshop, they must all put themselves in the customer's shoes and pretend that they are the customer (this is often easier said than done, but it is critical for the business and is perhaps the most important part of the whole exercise).

2. Start by completing (as a team), the first column of the template "Customer experience points." List in this column all key "touch-points" where your customers experience your business, its products, or services. Typical experience points for customers could be the initial purchase experience, ongoing service interactions, contacting your customer service, online transactions, and so on.

3. Once all common experience points are listed, take one experience point at a time and go all the way to the right of the template, one column at a time. The facilitator should moderate the discussion and help fill the template for each experience point.

4. Once the exercise is complete for customers who buy your company's products or service, it can be repeated for other stakeholders such as distributors, shareholders, employees or other internal customers, regulators, and so on.

5. The output of the strategic COPIS workshop is the complete "master list" of processes that the business needs to have and performance measures related to each process. The performance measures will be at three levels—voice of customer, process-related output measures, and in-process measures.

6. Before proceeding further, validate the outputs or findings of the workshop with real customers (maybe a sample of customers). This will help ensure that what we think is important for customers is actually so.

7. You now have the answers to two strategic questions: "What business processes do we need?" and "What to measure?" This is followed by detailed documentation/mapping and implementation on the ground of the processes thus identified. Actual adherence to each process is measured through process-compliance audits. These processes are also the foundation for continuous improvement in future.

8. Put in place the measurements identified through COPIS. The CEO and their leadership team must regularly review the actual performance trend on these measures. Often, the workshop generates a large number of measures—the CEO may select the top-priority (vital few) measures that they will personally review, while more detailed measures pertaining to each process must be monitored and reviewed by respective process owners.

9. Strategic COPIS can be applied with significant business benefit by new businesses at their inception stage or by existing businesses. For existing businesses, the COPIS workshop output must be used to validate their existing processes and performance measures.

**Figure 7** Step-by-step guide to using the strategic COPIS template.

new businesses right at inception, as well as by older businesses. For older businesses, the COPIS workshop output was used to validate their existing processes and performance measures. In fact, some of the older businesses realized after the strategic COPIS workshop that this was the first time in all their years of existence that they had stepped back to think about what processes and performance measures they actually needed. This helped them to validate and streamline their processes and put in place performance measures for the first time. During the last few years, some of the existing businesses have gone on from being just that—"existing" as one of the industry players—to become industry leaders—not merely in market share but in customer ratings as well. The strategic COPIS application has clearly contributed to this.

> *Strategic COPIS can be applied with significant business benefit by new businesses right at inception, as well as by older businesses.*

## FOUNDATION FOR CONTINUOUS IMPROVEMENT

In all the businesses, the processes identified through strategic COPIS have provided the foundation for continuous improvement. And the good news is that they don't even have to be perfect processes to begin with. In fact, several of the original processes have undergone changes over the years (this is the way it should be because processes are subject to continuous improvement). The process changes have often been triggered by less-than-desirable performance on the measures related to a process (including customer complaints). In many cases, a structured root cause analysis (following a defect or a complaint) or methods such as Lean or Six Sigma have been used for continuous improvement.

In several measures, performance has gradually but steadily improved over the years. This sustained and continuous improvement would not have been possible without the initial base of *relevant* business processes and performance measures that strategic COPIS gave each business.

In other words, we would have had nothing to improve without the initial base of business processes and performance measures. Strategic COPIS gave the businesses this base.

## BUSINESS BENEFITS OF STRATEGIC COPIS

The key benefits obtained by businesses applying strategic COPIS are:

- *Knowing what needs to be done and (equally important) avoiding what need not be done.* This was the most obvious benefit, and strategic COPIS helps achieve this by aligning business processes and performance measures with customer priorities. Each business got a complete master list of processes and performance measures that it needs, which helped them avoid unnecessary processes (bureaucracy) that could otherwise have crept in.

- *Strong cause-and-effect linkage between performance measures.* A business may have customer-related and internal/process-related performance measures, but often they tend to have just a bunch of measures without clear correlation with each other. This can be misleading and wasteful, as time and resources may be put into improving an internal measure that does not lead to improvement in customer experience. The strategic COPIS template forces a business to work "backward from the customer." Businesses that have implemented strategic COPIS are now experiencing a strong cause-and-effect linkage between different levels of performance measures related to the same process. In other words, the businesses are much more confident after applying strategic COPIS that, for any process, high process-compliance scores will result in high performance on internal/process-related measures, which in turn will result in fewer complaints and higher customer satisfaction scores. All of this, if sustained, contributes to edge over the competition and improved financial performance.

- *Employee KPIs.* The performance measures identified through COPIS are the primary source for identifying

employees' KPIs (key performance indicators, used for employee performance appraisals).
- *Customer-centric culture.* Being part of the strategic COPIS workshop and putting themselves in the customer's shoes is an experience that most participants don't forget for years. The use of the outward-in COPIS approach to identify organization-wide processes contributes to creating a customer-centric culture in the organization.

## OUTPUT OF STRATEGIC COPIS: MASTER LIST OF BUSINESS PROCESSES

The tangible output of the strategic COPIS exercise is the master list of processes that your business needs, and performance measures associated with each process. My experience has been that the number of business processes in companies I worked with typically ranged from around 60 to 100. We are talking of a comprehensive master list of processes, where not a single department or activity related to the business is left out. The only exceptions are one-time activities that are not likely to be repeated and hence don't need to be documented as standardized processes. Needless to say, there is nothing sacrosanct about the number of processes—it will differ from business to business; what is important is to ensure that: (a) processes have been identified from the customer's perspective (that's where the COPIS approach comes in), and (b) no important activity that needs to be done repeatedly gets left out of the master list.

The good news is that your master list does not have to be complete or perfect at the first go. It is always possible that a few processes get accidentally left out or become relevant a year or two down the line (that was our experience). What matters is that you have a continuous practice of updating the master list every time you find that an important process needs to be added. For that matter, it is also possible that a process that was relevant in the past may not be required anymore and needs to be removed from your master list. It is equally important to eliminate such obsolete processes from your master list.

A sample partial master list of processes for a company in the lending business is shown in Figure 8. As you will notice from Figure 8, processes have been organized under functions or departments.

| Department | Process owner | Process number | Name of process |
|---|---|---|---|
| Sales | Head of sales | S1 | Customer acquisition process |
| | | S2 | Lead management process |
| | | S3 | Distributor query and complaint resolution process |
| | | S4 | Distributor remuneration payout process |
| | | S5 | New distributor empanelment process |
| Products | Product head | P1 | New product development process |
| Risk management | Risk management head | CR1 | Underwriting and credit risk assessment process |
| Customer service | Customer service head | CS1 | Customer query and complaint resolution process |
| Operations | Operations head | O1 | Loan disbursement process |
| | | O2 | Post-disbursement operations process |
| Collection | Collections head | C1 | Asset repossession process |
| | | C2 | Collection process |
| HR | HR head | H1 | Recruitment process |
| | | H2 | Payroll process |
| | | H3 | Employee separation process |
| | | H4 | Employee learning and development process |
| | | H5 | Performance management process |
| Finance and accounting | CFO | | Finance and accounting processes |
| Technology | Technology head | | Technology processes |
| . . . and so on | | | |

**Figure 8** Sample (partial) master list of business processes identified through strategic COPIS.

However, this organization under departments was done *after* the processes were identified through the outside-in COPIS approach. Typically, one department "owns" several processes. The "process owner" is usually the head of the department. In companies I have worked with, many (in fact, most) processes cut horizontally across departments. I suspect that is the case in most companies. For example, in Figure 8, while "Loan disbursement" is the responsibility of the operations department, they would naturally be dependent on people from other departments (for example, sales) to do their job accurately and on time. This grouping of processes by function or department is primarily to ensure that a single owner is accountable to the customer (who receives the output of that process). These process owners, in turn, may need to have service-level agreements with their suppliers (suppliers could be other departments within the same company) for them to be able to deliver their promise to their customer.

## CONCLUSION

The experience of applying strategic COPIS at eight very different businesses for over eight years showed us that it gives clarity of direction and purpose to the business leaders as well as employees down the line. The strategic COPIS output provides everybody with the big picture that shows "What should we do?" (list of processes), "Why should we do it?" (processes are identified by working back from customer requirements), and "How do we know if we are doing it well?" (performance measures). It has helped the businesses focus on what is important to the customers and avoid waste by not doing what is not important to customers. In fact, some of the older businesses were able to actually question and eliminate stuff they had been doing for years after strategic COPIS showed them that it wasn't important to the customer—or anyone else, for that matter.

We now have a bunch of businesses that have actually let the customer decide what they should do (processes) and how their performance will be measured.

Clearly, we would have had no base for continuous improvement if the businesses had not applied strategic COPIS first. And finally, who can forget the experience of putting oneself in the customer's shoes?

Once you have created the master list of processes that your business needs (by applying the strategic COPIS approach), the next step is to actually map out or document how to do each process on your master list. We will look at this in the next chapter, through the story of Grandma Cakes!

# 5

# Standardize to Improve: Business Process Mapping

*Where there is no standard [process] there can be no kaizen [improvement]*

—Taiichi Ohno

We saw in the last chapter how we used the strategic COPIS approach to identify a master list of all processes that a company needs. The next step is to actually map out or document how to do each process on your master list.

When I first wrote this chapter, I used examples from businesses like insurance, auto manufacturing, hospitals, and commercial finance. On second thought, I replaced all that boring stuff with the delicious story of Grandma Cakes. I believe it will illustrate the concept equally well, and I hope you will enjoy the story at the same time. Here goes.

## GRANDMA CAKES

Years ago, when I was a university student in America, our little bunch of friends used to occasionally drop in at our buddy Brad's place. Brad had a lovely family, but they were going through difficult times. Brad's dad had been laid off and was looking for a new job. His mom worked as a temp. Brad worked part-time in a local store to help pay part of his tuition. His two little sisters were in school. And, last but not least, there was Brad's grandma Doris.

Grandma Doris was a big woman with a sharp tongue and a heart of gold. And her home-baked cakes were to die for. A visit to Brad's place was incomplete without generous helpings of grandma's cakes. Grandma was very popular at the local church, where she occasionally supplied cakes (the money from the sales went to charity). For the last couple of months, to help supplement the family income a bit, she had also started supplying cakes to the store where Brad worked. And, according to the store owner, customers loved them so much that Grandma's cakes flew off the shelf no sooner than they got there.

One afternoon, during a visit to Brad's place, a couple of us (with our mouths full of cake) half-seriously suggested to Grandma Doris that she should go into business on a larger scale and supply to more stores across the city. Grandma Doris, in her habitual loud voice, retorted, "You boys pulling my leg! Now have some more cake and get outta here!"

But Brad thought it was a good idea. "Why not, Grandma? After all, your cakes get sold out in no time at my store. I am sure they will also do well at other stores." Grandma chased us out of the house that day, but Brad didn't give up. Over the next few days, he was able to convince her that she should get into business. Always willing to help the family in their difficult time, Grandma finally agreed to give it a shot.

## EXPLOSIVE GROWTH—THE ARTISAN MULTIPLIES HERSELF

What happened next was amazing! In six months, Grandma was supplying her cakes to 20 stores across the city. In a year, about a hundred stores in the city and neighboring suburbs and towns were selling her cakes. Brad's parents now helped Grandma in her business, and they hired a few workers whom Grandma trained. In three years, Grandma Cakes had become an extremely popular brand sold at over 5000 stores in several cities. Their cakes were now made in eight factories. They employed about 400 people. The family was now comfortably well-off. Significantly, the quality of the cakes was almost the same as what Grandma used to make in her kitchen years ago. Only connoisseurs like Brad and me could tell the almost imperceptible difference. But I guess that is a small price that *had* to be paid in order for Grandma Doris, the artisan making a cake or two in her kitchen, to scale up to Grandma Cakes, the brand delivering thousands of consistent-quality cakes week after week, manufactured by hundreds of workers at eight factories in different cities.

## STANDARDIZED BUSINESS PROCESSES

How did this happen? No doubt Grandma was a magician at cake-making, but she couldn't be in all eight factories at the same time. So, Brad's dad did the next-best thing. At the auto parts factory where he used to work some years earlier, he had seen workers being trained on their work process. He had been part of some of the training programs himself. Usually, an experienced worker (an expert at the job) would train fresh or unskilled workers. Often, the company's training department would create training material that documented the process steps and explained them with the help of flow diagrams that would make it easy for the new workers to understand.

When the family's cake business started growing, Brad and his dad persuaded Grandma Doris to teach her way of cake-making to their first batch of workers. At first, Grandma refused to part with secret recipes she had learned from *her* grandma. But when Brad's dad made her understand that this was the only way they would be able to grow the business manifold, Grandma reluctantly agreed. As the growth continued and more workers and factories were added, Brad made a process map of the cake-making process with Grandma's help. On a sheet of paper, he wrote down exactly as his grandma told him, the step-by-step process of cake-making. He also wrote down the ingredients for each type of cake and other information needed for cake-making. Grandma and Brad trained a few of their older workers (who had by now picked up considerable experience in cake-making under Grandma's supervision) as trainers. These trainers would now use the process map to train new workers. Similarly, Brad and his dad documented other standard activities that happened repeatedly at their business. These included sales processes such as collecting orders and shipping cakes to stores, purchasing processes such as placing orders for ingredients or packing material and getting them delivered to Grandma's factories on time, and processes for calculating and paying salaries to the hundreds of people that Grandma Cakes employed.

## *WHO* NEEDS STANDARDIZED BUSINESS PROCESSES?

There is no cookie-cutter formula to define what type of organization needs standardized processes. A good rule of thumb could be any organization that has more than, say, 10 people, or more than a couple of locations where work happens. As we saw at Grandma Cakes, the moment the business grows to a size where one or a few individuals can not personally do all the work, but depend on more workers who are trained to do repetitive activities, it is a good idea to introduce standardized processes. By this definition, most small (except very tiny), medium, and large organizations—including businesses in *any* industry, government, and not-for-profit organizations—need standardized processes.

## THE PROCESS MAP

In businesses that I worked with, we used a standard format to document processes. One such format that I found especially useful was what we called a "four-sheeter"—simply because it has four sheets. If Grandma Cakes had used the four-sheeter format for documenting their cake-making processes, it would have looked something like the one shown in Figures 9 through 12. Of course, this is a simplified version shown for illustration purposes only (Grandma Doris would skin us alive if we revealed the full process to the public!).

The first sheet (see Figure 9) is a high-level overview of the process. It does not contain every single step in the process, but key milestones in the process. It also shows who the process owner is, what the output of the process is, how to measure whether the output is accurate and timely (as promised to the customer), what inputs the process owner requires, who will supply these inputs, and so on. For example, in the cake-making process, we assume that there are five key steps or milestones—mixing the ingredients, kneading, baking, cooling, and packing.

The second sheet (see Figure 10) is a graphical representation of the same process. Like the first sheet, it does not include every detailed step, but the flowchart format makes it easier for people to understand the overall process flow from start to end. While training people on how to do their jobs, we found the flowchart format useful to give them the big picture or an overview of the entire process before going into more minute details of the process steps.

Standardize to Improve: Business Process Mapping 47

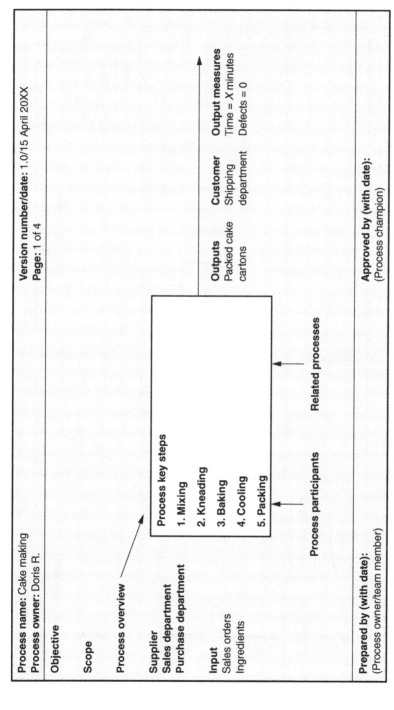

Figure 9 Sample process map (first sheet—process overview).

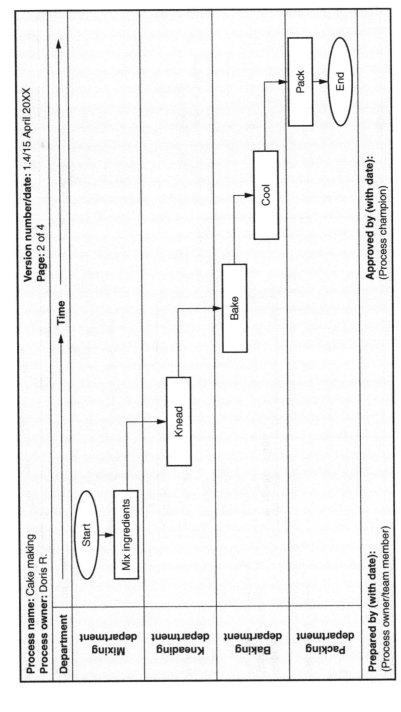

**Figure 10** Sample process map (second sheet—process flowchart).

**Process name:** Cake making
**Process owner:** Doris R.

**Version number/date:** 2.0/30 June 20XX
**Page:** 3 of 4

| Step description | Controls / Checks | Output of step | Customer | In-process measure | Responsibility |
|---|---|---|---|---|---|
| **1. Mixing** | | | | | |
| 1.1 Put ingredients in hopper | List of ingredients | | | | |
| 1.2 Mix ingredients in mixer | Mixer timer to 60 seconds | Mixed Ingredients | Kneading dept. | Time = Y seconds | Mixing dept. |
| 2. Knead | | | | | |
| 2.1 | | | | | |
| 2.2 | | | | | |
| 3. Bake | | | | | |
| 3.1 | | | | | |
| 3.2 | | | | | |
| 3.3 | | | | | |
| 4. Cool | | | | | |
| 4.1 | | | | | |
| 4.2 | | | | | |
| 5. Pack | | | | | |
| 5.1 Pack individual cake | | | | | |
| 5.2 Put cake in carton | | | | | |
| 5.3 Pack 24 cakes per carton | | | | | |

**Prepared by (with date):**
(Process owner/team member)

**Approved by (with date):**
(Process champion)

**Figure 11** Sample process map (third sheet—process details).

| Process name:<br>Process owner: | | | Version number/date: 1.0/15 April 20XX<br>Page: 4 of 4 | | | |
|---|---|---|---|---|---|---|
| Parameter | Performance measure | Target performance | Data source | Frequency of measurement | Responsibility for data | Who will review? |
| **Output measure**<br>*End to end measure*<br>Output measures are used to determine how well needs of the customer of the final output of the process are met<br><br>For example, end to end time taken from order receipt to delivery | Measure 1<br><br>Measure 2 | | | | | |
| **In-process measure**<br>*Measures that are internal to the process*<br>In-process measures are used to determine how well needs of the internal customer of each step in the process are met<br><br>For example, number of times kneading was defective | Measure 1<br><br>Measure 2 | | | | | |
| **Input measure**<br>Input measures are key quality and delivery requirements placed on your suppliers<br><br>For example, number of quality defects from an ingredient supplier | Measure 1<br><br>Measure 2 | | | | | |
| **Prepared by (with date):**<br>(Process owner/team member) | | | **Approved by (with date):**<br>(Process champion) | | | |

**Figure 12** Sample process map (fourth sheet—performance measures).

The third sheet (see Figure 11) contains the process details. It includes every single step and sub-step in the process. For example, in cake making, the first key step, "mixing," actually has two sub-steps, as shown in Figure 11. The third sheet also describes interim outputs (of key steps in the process). It identifies who the (internal) customer or recipient of each interim output is (the recipient of an interim output is usually not the end customer, but generally a person or department within the organization itself). For example, in cake making, the output of the first step, "mixing," is "mixed ingredients." The internal customer (recipient) of this output is the kneading department.

A couple of examples from other businesses: The internal customer (recipient) of a yet-to-be-painted car body in an automobile plant is the paint department. Or the internal customer of a bank loan application on which credit verification is to be done is the bank's credit verification department.

The third sheet also includes an important component of any process called "controls." A control is a rule that helps ensure that a process or a step in the process produces error-free (timely or accurate or both) output. In Grandma Cakes, the exact list of ingredients given by Grandma Doris is an example of a control. For your process to produce error-free output every time, your control has to work every time. You should try and see if you can implement *poka-yoke* (a Japanese term meaning *mistake-proofing*) to achieve this. Often, companies use technology to automate and mistake-proof their processes. For example, Grandma Doris's ever popular cinnamon oatmeal cake has to be baked at a particular temperature for an exact number of minutes. At Grandma Cakes factories, the ovens have temperature controls and timers built in that automatically ensure that there is no variation from the temperature and duration of baking. Our experience in businesses showed that there were many simple opportunities for mistake-proofing. Some of the best ideas for "*poka-yoke*-ing" a process come from the people who *do* that process. Some everyday examples of mistake-proofing are doors that will open only one way (to ensure that you don't flatten the nose of the person on the other side!) or a date field on a computer data entry screen that will only allow you to select a date from a calendar on the screen rather than type in the date.

The third sheet also describes "in-process" measures. For example, at Grandma Cakes factories, the target time to complete a batch of a particular variety of cake is 120 minutes end to end (output measure). This target for the output of the cake-making process can be achieved only if each step in the process is completed within the time allotted for that step. The number (or percentage) of batches in a day or month where the target time of 120 minutes was met is an example of an output measure of the entire process. The number (or percentage) of times where the target time for a particular step (say, mixing or kneading) was met is an example of an *in-process* measure. The *output measure* (for example, time taken to complete the full process, and quality of output of the full process) is dependent on the in-process measures (time taken to complete each interim step, and quality of output of each interim step).

Finally, the fourth sheet (see Figure 12) is a summary of the measures associated with the process. Most processes have (or should have) three types of performance measures—output measures, in-process measures, and input measures. We have already seen a brief explanation and examples of the first two types in the discussion on the third sheet above. *Input measures* are quality and delivery requirements for suppliers of the process; for example, for Grandma Cakes to be able to meet their promised delivery time and quality to the stores that sell their cakes, they would, in turn, need to have measurable quality and delivery-time agreements with their suppliers of ingredients.

As we saw in the last chapter, some businesses that I worked with had a total of 60 to 100 processes. Each one of these processes had a "four-sheeter" process document like the one shown in Figures 9 through 12.

## DO STANDARDIZED PROCESSES KILL INNOVATION? ON THE CONTRARY...

I don't know about you, but I have occasionally heard some people say that standardization can kill innovation. The irony is that these people were not terribly innovative themselves. I suspect that this is just a convenient excuse for those who do not want to submit to the discipline that standardized processes will enforce.

My actual experience in several businesses is the opposite. Almost no innovation or improvement is possible without standardization. Most innovation is an improvement of what already exists. In other words, you have nothing to improve unless you have *something* to improve. Sure, once every few years, some path-breaking idea that is truly "out of this world" may come along. But these are relatively rare, and, in any case, standardization doesn't stand in their way.

Having a standard and always being open to changing or improving it is the best way to progress. It is not standardization, but rigidity or refusal to change that gets in the way of innovation. Standardization actually makes continuous innovation possible. Progress is possible only if we have a standard and then continuously improve the standard.

> *Almost no innovation or improvement is possible without standardization . . . you have nothing to improve unless you have something to improve.*

> *Progress is possible only if we have a standard and then continuously improve the standard.*

Grandma Cakes was no different. Every so often, workers in the cake factories came up with ideas on a new variant of cake or a new ingredient that would increase their shelf life. Some store owners had suggestions on how to improve the packaging or how to reduce the shipping time from the factory to the stores. Each one of these innovative ideas was considered by Grandma Doris, Brad, and his parents, and quite a few of them were actually implemented. It was possible to quickly implement these improvements in a uniform way across all eight factories *only* because there already existed a standard process, into which each innovative idea was incorporated as a "process change." Once implemented, the innovation became part of the standard process at all factories—thus ensuring that its benefit was derived across the company. You may have noticed "version number" written on the top right corner of Figure 9. In many cases, a version change was the consequence of a process improvement resulting from an innovative idea.

As Henry Ford said, "Today's standardization is the foundation for tomorrow's improvement. If you think of 'standardization' as the best you know today, but which is to be improved tomorrow, you get somewhere. But if you think of standards as confining, then progress stops" (Liker 2004).

Making processes standardized does not mean they are cast in stone—as some people mistakenly seem to think. On the contrary, a standardized process is *expected* to be continuously improved. In fact, as Ford said, it can be improved *only* if the previous version was standardized in the first place. The new improvement also gives companywide and permanent benefit only if it becomes part of the next version of the standard process.

> *Making processes standardized does not mean they are cast in stone—as some people mistakenly seem to think. On the contrary, a standardized process is expected to be continuously improved.*

## WHY DO YOU NEED STANDARDIZED PROCESSES?

One of Toyota's famous 14 Principles is "Standardized tasks and processes." According to this principle, "Standardized tasks and processes are the foundation for continuous improvement and employee empowerment" (Liker 2004). The way that standardized processes are implemented at Toyota allows for continuous improvement—particularly from employees who actually *do* the process.

As we saw at Grandma Cakes (I've seen this at a number of other businesses as well), standardized processes are required for training people on their jobs. They also provide a base for continuous permanent improvement. Where processes are automated using technology, the standardized process document provides the basic map of "what to automate."

## YOU CAN HAVE YOUR OWN FORMAT FOR PROCESS MAPPING

The four-sheeter format for documenting processes is an example from some businesses where we used this particular format. Obviously, other companies don't need to follow the exact same format. What is important is that your business has *a* format for documenting your processes, and that your format contains key components like process steps, controls, process owner, performance measures, process output, and so forth, as discussed above.

## WHO SHOULD DOCUMENT PROCESSES?

Who hasn't heard of companies that hired a consultant to help them with process documentation? The consultant speaks to the people in the company who actually do the work. If the consultant is lazy, this discussion is done in a meeting room, without even going to the gemba (*gemba* is a Japanese word that means "the place where the work actually happens"). The consultant writes the company's processes as they are told to them and collects their fee. The impressive, thick process documents then gather dust on some shelf for years. A few years later, the same company blames the consultant for writing useless stuff.

However, to be fair, it's not entirely the consultant's fault. These companies either have no idea *why* they are creating such process documents, or they are doing it for the wrong reasons (a common wrong reason is to impress some auditor in the hope that the company will get an ISO 9001 Quality Management System certificate).

As opposed to this, look at Grandma Cakes. *Why* did Brad and his dad document their business processes? Because their business was growing, and they needed hundreds of workers at eight locations to do (on a large scale) what Grandma Doris used to do alone in her kitchen on a small scale. They realized that the only way they were going to be able to scale up quickly was to create standardized processes, document them, and teach this standardized way of working to the workers.

And *who* documented Grandma Cakes' processes? It was none other than Grandma Doris, the process owner herself. Alright, Brad may have typed out the document, but he took care to ensure that he documented what the expert—Grandma—told him. Unlike the consultant mentioned above, Brad was at the gemba and very much part of the process himself. Moreover, he did not document his own interpretation of the process. He made sure that the process document contained what the process owner, who actually knows the process best, told him.

At the same time, Brad and his dad had an important role to play—they brought in a standard format and ensured that *all* processes of the business were documented in the same format. As we saw, this turned out to be a blessing later, because they were able to quickly bring in innovations and improvements. Since the process format was standard, it was easy to incorporate such changes. It also helped them to "train the trainers," who, in turn, would train new workers. All this would have been rather chaotic if every process had a different format for documentation.

## HOW DO YOU KNOW IF PEOPLE ARE FOLLOWING THE STANDARD PROCESS?

We need to be clear that the main purposes of documented processes are to train people on their jobs, provide a basis for continuous improvement, and provide the source for automation—and *not* to satisfy some auditor. Companies sometimes show their process documents to auditors for ISO 9001 or other types of audit. Unfortunately, I have seen a few companies where this became an empty annual ritual—the process documents in these companies served no purpose other than being an exhibit for the auditors.

> *The main purposes of documented processes are to train people on their jobs, provide a basis for continuous improvement, and provide the source for automation— and not to satisfy some auditor.*

On the other hand, if done in the right spirit, *process-compliance audits* can serve a valuable purpose. Such an audit is nothing but an independent person (auditor) first understanding a process as defined by the process owner, and then going to the gemba to observe the process as it actually happens. The auditor then gives feedback to the process owner as to whether the process is being done on the ground the way the process owner (expert) *meant* it to be done.

In the early days when the cake business was small and they had just a handful of workers, Grandma Doris would personally go around checking if people were doing their jobs the way she had taught them (what a tongue-lashing they would get if they didn't!).

But as the business grew and more workers were employed, it became impossible for Grandma to go around supervising every worker. Brad and his dad introduced a system of process audits. Some of the experienced workers were trained as auditors. Such audits unearthed several useful opportunities to improve the process (for instance, a worker at one factory had found a better way to do their job—this just needed to be made part of the standard process to benefit the whole company) or identified workers who needed special training on their jobs.

## THE ROLE OF AUTOMATION AND THE NEED FOR WING-TO-WING THINKING

Automation can play a key role in ensuring compliance to a standardized process by eliminating human errors. It can also be used to capture and provide data for performance measures related to a process. However, it is important to remember that automation is not an end in itself. It should be seen as a means to deliver higher quality and speed to the customer at a lower cost through more-efficient processes. Also, my experience in several businesses was that while a large part or even all of what happened inside the company could be automated and controlled, the "first mile" and the "last mile" of many processes can be challenging. For example, much of the cake-making process within a Grandma Cakes factory is automated. However, for a large chain of stores (that is a customer of Grandma Cakes), the process begins the moment the store places an order with Grandma Cakes and ends when the cakes reach its shelves. The first mile is the order getting from the store to Grandma Cakes. The last mile is the cakes being shipped from the factory to the store. A frequent challenge with the first and last miles is that they may not be automated to the same extent or, in any event, not as much in the company's control as their own internal processes. However, the customer will still hold the company responsible end to end or "wing to wing"—and rightly so. Hence, companies need to figure out how best they can take care of the entire process, including the first and last mile, to the satisfaction of their customer. Because, after all, the only thing that the customer experiences is the end-to-end process. And it is based on this end-to-end experience that your customer will decide if they want to continue giving you their business.

> *The customer will still hold the company responsible end to end or "wing to wing" ... companies need to figure out how best they can take care of the entire process, including the first and last mile, to the satisfaction of their customer. Because, after all, the only thing that the customer experiences is the end-to-end process. And it is based on this end-to-end experience that your customer will decide if they want to continue giving you their business.*

## CONCLUSION

In this chapter, I have made an attempt to make the vital topic of business process standardization and mapping easy and, I hope, even enjoyable reading through the story of Grandma Cakes. The contents of this chapter are equally relevant to your company, whether you are in manufacturing or insurance or banking or education or healthcare or hospitality or government or almost any other type of organization.

Along with mapping the steps in a process, collecting and analyzing data and performance measurements are an equally important part of managing your processes, and your business. In the next chapter, we will look at different types or "layers" of performance measurement, and how to select the "measures that matter."

# 6
# Measures that Matter

*In God we trust—all others bring data.*
—W. Edwards Deming

In the last chapter, we saw how to standardize and map or document your business processes so that they give you a base for continuous improvement. Now, how do you know what your current level of performance is, and whether your performance is improving compared to last quarter or last year, and compared to the competition? That's where data and performance measurements come in. Performance measurement is an equally important part of managing your processes, and your business. In this chapter, we will look at different types or "layers" of performance measurement through an interesting story.

Traditional performance measures—usually financial outcomes—are "after the event." They tell us how we did last month or last quarter, but are of little use in predicting future performance. This chapter talks about four layers of performance measures—financial outcomes being the outermost layer. As we move from "outside in," or from outcomes to enablers, we find that the performance measures get increasingly easier to control. Then, if we work on the enablers, the outcomes become more predictable. Provided, of course, that we have ensured a strong cause-and-effect relationship between each layer and the next.

## 60  Chapter Six

> *Traditional performance measures—usually financial outcomes—are "after the event." They tell us how we did last month or last quarter, but are of little use in predicting future performance.*

And now the story.

Joy returned to his office in a bad mood. "Call the team to my office for an emergency meeting. Ask everyone to drop whatever they are doing and come *now*," he barked at his secretary as he entered his office. Joy is CEO of a large insurance company. He was just back from a board meeting where he had been grilled about his company's falling market share and profits in the auto insurance business.

Ten minutes later, the senior management team was in his office. Joy asked them the same questions that he had been asked by the board that morning. "The board has warned us that if we don't shape up, we might have to shut shop soon." Addressing the sales head, Naom, he added, "Naom, clearly, you will have to sell more insurance policies to get us out of this spot."

Naom: "But the whole industry is in a decline. The competition is intense. We can sell more only if we significantly reduce our premium rates."

Joy: "You know we can't afford to do that! Our profits are already falling. Reducing rates is only going to increase our losses."

Naom: "Some of our largest competitors are undercutting everybody on price. Obviously, they are taking losses as well, but seem to be intent on taking the entire industry down with them."

Joy: "Doesn't anybody have any ideas?"

Anup, the marketing head, had one, "I think we should have a big advertising campaign on TV. You can't expect sales to go up if you don't spend enough on advertising."

Joy: "Given our recent performance, we can't even afford to advertise on *radio*, let alone TV. I was looking for ideas on how we can make money, not spend money, which we don't have anyway!"

This was followed by some general murmurs among the team—". . . they won't let us reduce prices, they won't spend on advertising . . . how do they expect us to increase sales?"

For a few minutes everybody stared blankly at the large screen, which had a slide showing the (rather dismal) numbers that Joy had presented at the board meeting earlier in the day.

Dev, a senior executive who had recently joined the company, broke the silence. "What other performance measures do we have?" Barak, the CFO, looked at Dev impatiently, "Whaddya mean 'other performance measures'? We measure our premium revenue, expenses, claims paid, profits—rather, in our case, losses—pretty much what every company in the industry monitors."

Dev: "Pardon my saying so, but these are outcomes or 'after the event' measures. They tell us how well—or how not-so-well—we did last quarter or last year. But they tell us nothing about *why* we did badly. Nor do they give us any suggestion as to how to improve going forward. Do we have any measures that will help us *predict* future performance? To begin with, do we know *why* we lost market share?"

Naom: "That's easy. We sold fewer policies than we did last year. We're not able to add enough new customers. Worse, many of our existing customers are not renewing their insurance with us. That's what beats me; after all, we are cheaper than the competition!"

Dev: "That's interesting. But how come a few of our competitors are doing well in the same markets? They don't charge higher premiums than we do, nor have any of them had any major advertising campaign."

Naom looked at Dev. He knew that Dev was right. "I wonder why customers go to them. Our products are similar, our prices are, if anything, better, yet we keep losing our customers to them."

Dev: "That should be possible to find out. Why don't we ask our customers?"

Some of the veterans rolled their eyes toward the ceiling. *Now* what was this young upstart trying to teach them?

Ram, the customer service head, who had been silent so far, now spoke. "I think Dev has a point. In fact, our customers are already speaking to us; we just need to start listening."

Joy looked interested, but puzzled. "Can you make yourself clear, Ram?"

Ram responded by asking, "Naom, what is the biggest USP (unique selling proposition) for any company in the car insurance business?"

Naom: "That would be claims. Most customers buy insurance for peace of mind, and they would like to know that they can depend on their insurance company should they have a claim."

Ram: "Precisely. Now, in our case the largest number of complaints we get from our customers is about claims. In fact, three out of every 10 customers who experience a claim actually write or call us to complain. Our data show that a significant percentage of our customers are not happy with our speed or accuracy in processing claims."

Dev: "So the complaints data is one type of measure that tells us the 'voice of the customer'—if we are ready to listen. Another way of measuring customer voice could be a customer satisfaction survey."

Ram: "We actually did a customer satisfaction survey six months ago. It was even benchmarked with some of our key competitors. The results again showed that our customers rated us way below on 'claims experience' than competitors were rated by *their* customers. I had e-mailed the survey report to you all."

Joy: "I am sure that for every customer who formally complains to us, there are several who just take their business elsewhere. Besides, I imagine many unhappy customers must also be telling their friends about their bad experience with our company. That doesn't exactly work wonders for our reputation. In our business, if you don't build a reputation of trust, customers will leave you, even if you are the cheapest. If only we—the senior management—had paid more attention to the customer complaints and satisfaction scores and improved the claims process last year, we wouldn't have lost so many customers."

Dev: "In other words, customer-related measurements like complaints data and customer satisfaction scores would have helped us to *predict* and improve the business outcome of market share. As Joy said, not every unhappy customer complains. Most of them just walk out on us. It may, therefore, help to have one more type of performance measure, which would help us to detect *every* defective transaction, irrespective of whether the customer complained or not. For example, what percentage of all claim settlements are delayed or inaccurate? For this, we would have to set our own internal performance targets or service standards and measure each transaction against this standard. For example, if our internal target time to settle a car insurance claim is 15 days, and we receive a thousand claims in a month, what percentage of them were actually settled in 15 days—

irrespective of whether the customer complained or not? This is an internal, or process-related, measure that would help us to *predict* our performance on customer-impacting processes. I did a quick check on our claims for the last two months. As much as 35% of the claims we receive are not settled within 15 days . . ."

Chan, the claims head, interrupted, "But most of that could be the customer's fault. You should know that in a large number of claims, the customers delay sending us the documents necessary to process the claim. Surely, you can't blame the claims department for that."

Joy intervened, "Relax, Chan. Nobody is trying to blame you. We are not even interested in fixing the blame on anybody, as that is not going to help our business to improve. We are merely discussing how we can get to know about business problems or *potential* business problems as early as possible so that we can do something about them *before* they impact our customers and our business."

Dev continued, "Process-related measures are of three types—output, input, and in-process measures. In our example, timely settlement of claims is an 'output' of the claims process, and hence percentage of claims settled on time is an *output measure*. A major process such as claims has several steps or subprocesses. For example, to pay a car insurance claim within 15 days, we may need the customer's claim form along with supporting documents to reach our office within seven days of the customer first initiating the claim. Percentage of claim forms with accurate documents received within seven days would then be an *input measure*. By the way, in a random sample that I studied, we received 70% of the claim forms with accurate documents within seven days. For processes with many steps, there could be some additional measures of timeliness or accuracy along key milestones within the process. Such measures are called *in-process measures*. Input and in-process measures help us *predict* our performance on the output measure."

Joy: "Dev, this is interesting, and you've got us thinking. But I still have a question. Clearly, the customer- and process-related measures would help us detect defects such as customer complaints or delayed claim settlements before they translate into reduced market share. However, though they happen earlier in the chain than lost market share, in one sense, they are also 'after the event' in that they tell us about defects *after* defects happen. What I mean is that like 'lost market share,' a complaint or a delayed claim payment is also a defect. Is there a way we can predict them even earlier in the chain and reduce even these types of 'internal defects,' if I may call them that? After all, the earlier a defect or symptom is detected, the easier it would be to correct."

Dev: "Sure we can. You might have heard of something called a *process-compliance audit*. Remember, all our critical business processes are documented. A process document shows the key steps in the process, who should do each step, performance measures with targets for key milestones within the process, and controls or rules to produce error-free output. We have such a document for our claims process as well. A process compliance audit will tell us to what extent the documented process is being followed on the ground. Assuming the process is designed to produce output of the required quality and within the time required by the customer, the higher the process compliance, the lower the subsequent defects are likely to be. Process compliance audit scores can actually be measured. Higher process compliance audit scores are likely to result in higher performance on in-process and output measures of the process."

Chan: "I must admit, you may have a point. Some years ago, when our company was smaller, we had fewer claims and fewer people handling them. We had a few experienced people in the claims department. I knew each of them personally and could rely on their knowledge and experience. We had hardly any need for formal documented processes. However, in the last few years the market has grown manifold, so has our company, and, naturally, so has the number of claims. We now have over a hundred people processing claims at our offices all over the country. Moreover, with intense competition, we keep losing good employees to other companies. We have to replace them with new people. We have reached a size and scale where we can not depend just on the excellence of individuals any more. We need to have standardized processes and train all our people on our processes."

Joy: "Sounds good, Chan. We should also implement the process compliance audits that Dev was talking about. After all, what good is a process that merely exists on paper, but isn't followed?"

Pat, the HR manager, who had been listening intently, said, "To summarize, Dev spoke about four 'layers' of performance measures (see Figure 13). Moving "outside in," or from outcomes to enablers, the outermost layer is the 'business' or financial outcomes, the next inner layer is customer voice, followed by internal or process-related measures, and the innermost layer is process compliance audit scores. If we can make sure that there is a strong cause-and-effect relationship between each layer and the next, we should be

## Measures that Matter 65

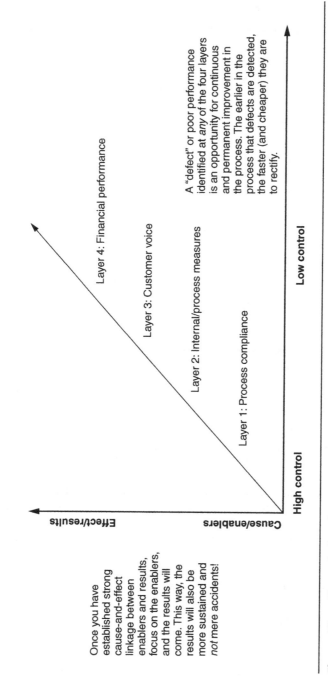

**Figure 13** "Layers" of performance measures.

able to predict and influence outcomes by measuring and acting on the enablers in advance. I think we need to change our performance appraisal system. Today, our employees' performance is mostly measured and rewarded on financial outcomes like sales revenue. We should also have measures from the other three layers on their performance appraisals. For example, a salesperson (who is today measured purely on their sales numbers, that is, layer 4) would also receive points on their appraisal for customer satisfaction scores and customer complaints on the sales experience (layer 3), internal measures such as percentage of sales applications that were right and complete the first time (layer 2), and adherence to the sales process measured through process compliance audits (layer 1)."

## TWO YEARS LATER

Joy the CEO floated into his office. "Call the team. Can you also order some tea and snacks?" He was just back from another board meeting. His secretary hadn't failed to notice that, of late, Joy returned from board meetings in great spirits.

And why not? The company's performance had significantly turned around. Revenue, profits, and market share have all picked up slowly but steadily during the last five quarters. Customer satisfaction ratings have been looking up. Most importantly, people in the company feel that they are more in control of their outcomes. In the bad old days, outcomes would just happen to them, and they wouldn't have a clue as to what was to be done. All that now seemed to be a thing of the distant past.

Two years ago, they had introduced the new "holistic" performance measurement system. The company's and employees' performance was measured using a combination of measures from all four layers. There had been initial resistance from some people, but the skeptics were either persuaded or forced to fall in line. It had taken a couple of quarters to fine-tune the measures and ensure proper cause-and-effect linkage between the "outcomes" in layers 4 and 3 and the "enablers" in layers 2 and 1.

"The boys on the board now want us to help them introduce our system in other companies in the group. The regulator called me for a meeting last week. I am not ashamed to admit now that I went there with some trepidation. To my surprise, even they seem to have heard about our performance measurement system. They wanted to know how they can get other companies in the industry to follow our system. For the first time in my years in the industry, I came away from a meeting with the regulator without having my ears chewed off . . . another cup of tea, Dev?"

## THE DASHBOARD REVIEW

The substance of this chapter is that traditional measures of financial "outcomes" such as revenue and profit, while important, are clearly not adequate for top management focus. We need other types of performance measures that are not merely "after the event" but will help us to actually predict and improve our outcomes. In other words, "enablers"—also sometimes called *leading indicators* (as opposed to outcomes, which are *lagging indicators*). We looked at four layers of performance measures.

More importantly, it is not enough to just have a disjointed bunch of measures under the four layers; we need to ensure that there is a strong cause-and-effect relationship between performance measures in one layer and the next. "Defects" or poor performance identified at *any* level or layer is an opportunity for improving the process. However, the earlier in the process that defects are detected, the easier (and, usually, cheaper) they are to correct. For example, in the insurance company in this story, the company losing revenue due to customers leaving (layer 4) *or* customers leaving the company due to a poor claims experience (layer 3) are relatively more difficult to resolve than if the problem had been detected earlier—say, at the stage where an employee in the claims department, due to lack of proper training on their job, was causing delays in processing claims (layer 1). This could have been easily fixed by training the employee. The parallel with medical science and the importance of detecting and treating a disease early is hard to miss.

> *"Defects" or poor performance identified at any level or layer is an opportunity for improving the process. However, the earlier in the process that defects are detected, the easier (and, usually, cheaper) they are to correct.*

And most importantly, the CEO or business head needs to personally review important measures in *all four* layers related to their critical business processes. I have had the pleasure of working with some business leaders who (after having established strong cause-and-effect linkages between enablers and outcomes) would focus more on the enablers (layers 1, 2, and 3) with supreme confidence that the results would follow. In my experience, such leaders usually end up achieving bigger and more sustained results.

In businesses that I worked with, we started a monthly "dashboard" review of performance measures related to key business processes. The CEO and leadership team of a business participate in the dashboard review. A typical dashboard shows performance on all four layers for one critical process, and we make sure that all important processes that impact customers or the business are personally reviewed by the CEO. An example of such a dashboard for the insurance claims process in the story is shown in Figure 14. The data sources and recommended frequency for each "layer" of performance measurement are shown in Table 1.

In several businesses, I had an opportunity to participate in dashboard reviews that were conducted month after month without missing a single month for years. Quite a few CEOs who led their companies to significant and sustained business success and edge over competition acknowledged the role of the dashboard review and the focus and improvement actions resulting from it as important contributors to the sustained success of the business.

In helping companies implement such a "balanced" performance measurement system, I have drawn much inspiration from the *balanced scorecard* concept (Kaplan and Norton 1992).

In this chapter and the previous one, we looked at the need to lay a foundation of standardized businesses processes and performance measures. Without this foundation, no improvement or progress is possible. Now that we have the foundation of processes and performance measures, and a mechanism in the form of the dashboard review to assess our performance regularly, let us look at "how to improve" our performance. That is the subject of the next few chapters.

*Measures that Matter* 69

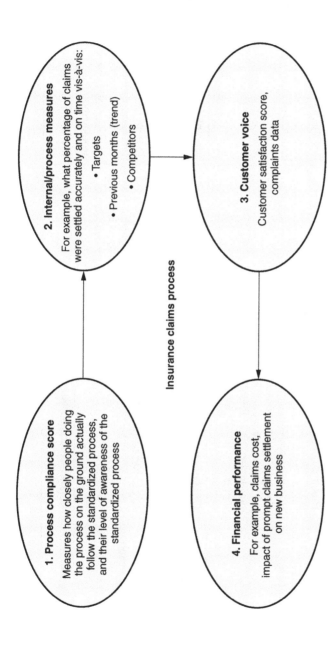

**Figure 14** Sample 360-degree quality dashboard.

**Table 1** Data sources and recommended frequency for each layer of performance measurement.

| Layer | Data source | Frequency of measurement | Frequency of review by senior management |
|---|---|---|---|
| 1. Process compliance score | Process compliance audits | Monthly/quarterly or continuous | Monthly/quarterly |
| 2. Internal/process measures | Business systems/logs (for automated processes, it has to be ensured while developing the automation that required data will be captured) | Continuous | Monthly or more frequent |
| 3a. Customer voice (Complaints data) | CRM or other system used for recording and tracking customer complaints | Continuous | Monthly or more frequent (respective process owners to review complaints pertaining to their own processes daily) |
| 3b. Customer voice (Customer satisfaction scores) | Customer satisfaction survey | Quarterly/annual (quick feedback on a specific experience could be instant or part of the process itself) | Quarterly/annual (implementation of improvement actions following each survey to be reviewed weekly/monthly) |
| 4. Financial performance | Financial/management accounting reports | Continuous | Monthly |

# 7
# The Beginning of Improvement: Making Quality Problems Visible

*You can't improve what you can't see.*

So far in this book, we have looked at how to lay the foundation for continuous permanent improvement. The pillars of this foundation are a shared purpose and direction (in the form of the business excellence road map aligned with your business strategy), standardized business processes, and performance measures.

I have seen several companies jump to the more "glamorous" aspects of business excellence, such as Six Sigma quality improvement programs, without creating this foundation. This is like trying to erect a tall building without first laying a foundation underground. Like this building, such programs are bound to collapse. In my experience, the foundation-laying phase is relatively low-profile work (some people may even find it boring) but most important. As I never tire of saying, no improvement is possible—or at least, no *permanent* improvement is possible—without this foundation.

---

*In my experience, the foundation-laying phase is relatively low-profile work (some people may even find it boring) but most important. As I never tire of saying, no improvement is possible—or at least, no permanent improvement is possible—without this foundation.*

---

Of course, every improvement project is expected to go back to the process and make the foundation even stronger than before (by making the improvement a permanent part of the process), but you need *a* foundation to begin with.

Now that you have put the foundation in place, let us look at *how to improve* our performance. That is the subject of this and the next few chapters.

## MEASUREMENT ITSELF CAUSES IMPROVEMENT

It was our experience that merely starting to measure and review performance—especially on quality- and customer-related measures—led to one level of improvement in performance on several measures, even before we took any specific improvement actions. Colleagues and acquaintances from several other organizations have shared the same experience. This is not surprising because the performance dashboards help focus the organization's attention on these critical measures, and make hitherto hidden quality problems visible.

## WHERE TO BEGIN IMPROVEMENT— START BY MAKING QUALITY PROBLEMS VISIBLE

One of the quality principles of Toyota from which I draw much inspiration and try my best to help companies implement is to make quality problems visible (Liker 2004). Based on years of experience in quality improvement programs, I am completely convinced that the starting point of quality improvement is to make quality problems visible. After all, how can we improve what we can not see?

> *The starting point of quality improvement is to make quality problems visible. After all, how can we improve what we can not see?*

A quality problem can be anything from a defective part supplied by a vendor, to a defective product produced at your factory, to a customer complaint about shoddy service. Quality problems, to my mind, are not "problems," but opportunities for continuous permanent improvement. Wouldn't it then be foolish to lose these opportunities? Does your company have a culture where employees on the ground feel genuinely encouraged to make quality problems visible? Or is the culture one where people feel the need to hide quality problems from their boss? The hiding culture generally develops in organizations where the practice is to *blame* somebody for quality problems, rather than try to find out the root cause of the problem so that we can improve. It is the responsibility of senior management to convince employees down the line that making quality problems visible is a behavior that is expected and genuinely appreciated. Why can't we reward employees who make quality problems visible, and demonstrate to employees that we are not interested in knowing *who* is to blame, but most interested in knowing *what* the root cause of the problem is and *how* to prevent it in future? Employees—especially those on the ground who are in touch with customers—are your organization's eyes and ears. If you shut them up, you are shutting your eyes and ears to your customers—and we all know what happens to companies that do this. On the other hand, empower your people to uncover quality problems fearlessly and involve them in finding out the root cause and preventing the problem—and see the difference.

So, the first step in beginning to improve performance is to make quality problems visible. After all, you can't solve problems that remain hidden from you, or that you choose to hide from! And trust me when I tell you that if you have successfully created an organizational culture where people feel genuinely encouraged to make quality problems visible, you already have a significant advantage over many of your competitors, and you've moved a huge step toward continuous permanent improvement. So, if you're the CEO or part of the leadership team, work on creating and nurturing this culture.

> *If you have successfully created an organizational culture where people feel genuinely encouraged to make quality problems visible, you already have a significant advantage over many of your competitors, and you've moved a huge step toward continuous permanent improvement.*

## CLEAR THE COBWEBS WITH 5S

We found the simple technique of 5S (see Table 2) a useful first step in clearing the way for application of other performance improvement techniques such as Lean and Six Sigma (siliconfareast.com 2004). 5S is a systematic program to achieve cleanliness, order, and standardization in the workplace. A well-organized workplace results in more efficient and more productive operation. 5S helped us by clearing the clutter and cobwebs—from the physical workplace, from computers, from our minds—again helping to make quality problems visible. While some people associate 5S with manufacturing and factories, our experience has taught us that it is equally relevant and useful in *any* industry, including services.

From factories covered with dirt, to offices with piles of paper reaching the ceiling, to computers with data and applications that pertain to everything except what you need for your work—all these are examples of a work environment where visibility to elements relevant to your work is poor, making it easy for quality problems to remain hidden—until they reach your customers (now, you don't want *that* to happen, do you?) 5S, by helping to get rid of stuff that you don't require for your work, and then properly organizing what you *do* require, makes your work environment clutter-free and more visible, thus helping you to work better, and also making any quality problems immediately visible.

Table 2    5S definitions.

| 5S term | Explanation |
| --- | --- |
| Sort (make tidy) | Throw away all rubbish and unrelated materials in the workplace |
| Straighten (or set in order) | Set everything in proper place for quick retrieval and storage (a place for everything and everything in its place) |
| Shine (cleanliness) | Clean the workplace |
| Standardize | Standardize the way of maintaining order and cleanliness |
| Sustain | Make 5S a regular practice; discipline |

Note: The original Japanese equivalents for the above five terms in the same sequence (top to bottom) are *seiri, seiton, seiso, seiketsu,* and *shitsuke.*

Source: www.siliconfareast.com/5S.htm.

## LISTEN TO CUSTOMER COMPLAINTS AND LOOK AT YOUR PERFORMANCE MEASURES

The most important purpose of establishing performance measurements, as we saw in the last chapter, is to make quality problems visible—so that we can improve them. We found our performance dashboards to be a great place to look for quality problems or defects.

Ideally, quality problems should be detected, corrected, and prevented *before* they reach the customer. However, if some of them do manage to slip through and actually reach the customer, usually some customers are kind enough to bring them to our attention. We found customer complaints to be another excellent source of opportunities for continuous permanent improvement.

> *We found customer complaints to be another excellent source of opportunities for continuous permanent improvement.*

Once the basic culture of making quality problems visible is established, people in the organization can actually be trained on certain simple but highly effective techniques of *how* and *where* to look for waste and other opportunities for improvement. We will look at these in the next chapter.

# 8
# The Fascinating World of Lean

*Lean is a way to do more and more with less and less.*

—James Womack

My friend Ajit once jokingly said, "I formerly had a boss who often used to call me *muda*. For some time, I thought this was a compliment. Till someone told me what it means."

The boss had worked for some years with Toyota, and *muda* is a Japanese term that means *waste*.

Near-obsession with waste and its elimination is one of the main qualities that struck me about Toyota, the Lean philosophy, and, for that matter, about Japan. Have you noticed how elegantly simple many things about Japan and the Japanese are? I suspect this has something to do with Lean thinking, which seems to be embedded in the Japanese psyche.

## LEAN IS FOR SENIOR MANAGEMENT FIRST

The experience of implementing Lean in several large and diverse businesses over several years taught us that Lean is not merely a set of methods or tools, but, more importantly, an organization-wide strategy, mind-set, and culture. If some readers would like me to define Lean, I look at Lean as an organization-wide mind-set of continuously looking for waste reduction and sustainable cost savings opportunities that benefit the company as well as customers. In fact, it gives much more substantial and sustained business results if senior management believes in Lean in this broader sense. Lean is as much for senior management as it for employees on the shop floor.

> **Lean is as much for senior management as it for employees on the shop floor.**

Some companies have "Lean departments." Frankly, I find this quite ridiculous. Does it mean everybody else in the company can afford to be flabby and wasteful? Lean can and does make a significant difference if it becomes the way the organization and all of its people think and work.

This book does not purport to be a complete text on Lean or the Toyota Production System. There are several excellent books on these that students of quality (including me) must read and help organizations implement. The main purpose of this book is to tell the story of how we *applied* Lean and other quality principles in diverse businesses, in the hope that others can benefit from our experience.

In this chapter, I will share examples of some of the Lean techniques that businesses that I worked with actually implemented with remarkable results. These were implemented in a variety of businesses from different industries by average people. Hence, I thought it would be useful to share, as almost any company would find them relatively easy to implement, and yet derive significant results. If we could do it, you can do it!

## IDENTIFYING AND ELIMINATING WASTE (THE NINE TYPES OF WASTE)

We began our Lean journey by training selected batches of employees on the types of waste. Several texts talk about seven or eight types of waste; we added one or two of our own. The nine types of *muda*, or waste, can be easily remembered by the mnemonic or acronym "DOWNTIMER." Each character is the first letter of the name of a type of waste. The nine types of waste and examples of each are:

1. *Defects in products or service.* For example, production of defective products, an error by a bank on a customer's account statement, an incorrect or incomplete sales order brought in by a salesperson. All this results in avoidable (wasteful) repair, rework, replacement, and complaint handling.
2. *Overproduction/consumption.* For example, producing items for which there are no orders, producing sales application forms or marketing material far in excess of what is used, avoidable electricity or travel costs.
3. *Waiting time.* For example, waiting between process steps, or because of stock-outs or slow computers or systems being down, and so on.
4. *Non-utilized people.* For example, inactive employee time or even losing opportunities to benefit from employees' ideas by not listening to them.
5. *Transport.* Avoidable/excess movement of material.
6. *Inventory.* For example, excess raw materials, finished goods, application forms, marketing material, or administrative supplies.
7. *Motion.* Any excess/avoidable movement of people.
8. *Excess processing.* For example, unnecessary process steps, fields on application forms that are never used, return envelopes provided for loan repayments to customers who pay electronically, unnecessary multiple approvals.
9. *Reinventing the wheel.* For example, good practices in certain pockets of the organization (or, for that matter, outside—including at competitors) that are not replicated. (Liker 2004)

Table 3 shows in detail the nine types of waste with examples, the cost of each type of waste, and how to avoid it.

In our experience, the types of waste don't need to be memorized by employees. We found that the best way to get results is to train employees on the types of waste, and then use them as a checklist to look at their own work processes on their job and see if one or more types of waste exist.

**Table 3** DOWNTIMER: the nine types of *muda* or waste.

| Type of waste | Examples | Avoidable cost due to this waste | How to avoid this waste |
|---|---|---|---|
| 1. Defects in products or service | Production of defective products, an error by a bank on a customer's bank account statement, an incorrect or incomplete sales order brought in by a salesperson | Cost of repair, rework, replacement, and complaint handling | Design processes that produce error-free output; use poka-yoke or mistake-proofing; train people to do their jobs right the first time |
| 2. Over production/ consumption | Producing items for which there are no orders, producing sales application forms or marketing material far in excess of what is used, avoidable energy or travel costs | Cost of producing, storing, wastage/ spoilage | Use "pull" wherever possible; produce only what is required; develop just-in-time capability |
| 3. Waiting time | Waiting between process steps or due to stock-outs or due to slow computers or systems being down | Cost of idle people and equipment | *Heijunka*, or leveling; multiskilling of employees |
| 4. Non-utilized people | Inactive employee time or losing opportunities to benefit from employees' ideas by not listening to them | Cost of idle people and opportunity cost of lost ideas and improvements | Create an organizational culture of encouraging people to come up with ideas and implementing them; heijunka, or leveling; multiskilling of employees |
| 5. Transport | Avoidable/excess movement of material | Cost of transport and overall excess process time | Design the workplace to ensure that minimum transport is required |

*Continued*

Table 3  Continued.

| Type of waste | Examples | Avoidable cost due to this waste | How to avoid this waste |
|---|---|---|---|
| 6. Inventory | Excess raw materials, finished goods, application forms, marketing material, administrative supplies | Cost of storage, obsolescence, damage. Excess inventory also masks or hides inefficiencies | Use 'pull' wherever possible; carry minimum possible inventory; develop 'just-in-time' capability |
| 7. Motion | Excess/avoidable movement of people | Cost of movement and overall excess process time | Design the workplace to ensure minimum movement is required |
| 8. Excess processing | Unnecessary process steps, fields on application forms that are never used, return envelopes provided for loan repayments to customers who pay electronically, unnecessary multiple approvals | Cost of extra processing, which customers don't value | Avoid excess processing. Think if you would be willing to pay for this extra processing, if you were the customer |
| 9. Reinventing the wheel | Good practices in certain pockets of the organization (or, for that matter, outside—including at competitors) that are not replicated | Cost of not having the best practice at all, or extra time and cost spent in "reinventing" something that could have been quickly just "copied" | Create culture, systems and processes that encourage and enable employees to share and replicate relevant knowledge and best practices from within and outside |

> *We found that the best way to get results is to train employees on the types of waste, and then use them as a checklist to look at their own work processes on their job and see if one or more types of waste exist.*

## WHAT WE LEARNED FROM TOYOTA

In some companies that I had an opportunity to work with, we wanted to be the "Toyota" of our industry. How close we came to Toyota could be debated, but without a doubt, the attempt brought clear business and cultural benefits. Some of the key Toyota principles that we made a genuine attempt to emulate are as follows:

- *Long-term philosophy.* Basing management decisions on a long-term philosophy even at the cost of short-term financial goals. In cultures and companies that are unable to follow this fully (I suspect this would be the case with a number of organizations across the world), a second-best, but practical, approach may be to create what I call an "outer wheel and inner wheels." While the larger and slower outer wheel represents medium- to long-term goals, inner wheels are quick hits or intermediate results that give benefits in the short term as well as provide continued motivation to work on the long term. However, it is important to avoid things that could be seemingly beneficial in the short term but actually harm the organization's long-term goals. For example, palming off poor-quality products or cheating customers may help bring in some revenue this quarter, but is clearly going to harm your long-term goals.

- *FTR (first time right).* Enabling every employee to do their job right the first time, every time.

- *Building quality into processes.* Building quality into your processes so that your processes produce quality outputs (products or service). This principle includes continuously improving the process.

- *Customer-first or outside-in approach.* Putting oneself in the customer's shoes.

- *Heijunka.* Leveling the workload (as far as possible) to avoid having peaks and troughs during the day, month, quarter, or year.
- *Jidoka.* Stopping to fix problems. This includes immediate correction, root cause analysis, and preventive action (process improvement).
- *Andon.* Making quality problems visible (or drawing attention to quality problems) so that they can be addressed.
- *Standardized processes.* The foundation for continuous improvement.
- *Kaizen (continuous improvement).* Defects, customer complaints, and performance dashboards are great sources of continuous improvement. The approach on detecting defects or complaints must be *not* to fix the blame, but to fix the problem and prevent recurrence.
- *Use appropriate technology appropriately.* Use technology that will help your processes to work better or reduce costs; don't bring in technology for technology's sake.
- *Genchi genbutsu.* Go to the place where the work actually happens and see for yourself "rather than theorizing based on what other people or the computer screen tell you." This is applicable to senior management as well.

(Note: This is a partial list selected from Toyota's Fourteen Principles that we actually worked on implementing. In a literal sense, *jidoka* and *andon* have slightly more specific meanings in a manufacturing context, but their broader meaning as applicable to any industry is given above. We tried to implement them in this broader sense.)

## VALUE STREAM MAPPING—AUTOBIOGRAPHY OF A SALES ORDER

So far in this chapter, we have talked a lot about waste. But what exactly is waste? Obviously, something that does not add value. Value to whom? To the customer, of course. Now, that brings us to the question of what is value. Before answering this question, let us look at the autobiography of a sales order.

The autobiography: Hi, I am a sales order. You know—the piece of paper or computer screen on which the customer describes what they want to buy, and how much, and hands it over to the seller. We sales orders are quite common, whether you want to buy a car or a television or insurance, or apply for a loan—or pretty much anything (you can think of the product or service that customers buy from your company). I was born one morning when a salesperson met a customer. The customer wrote me out and handed me over to the salesperson. Took about 30 minutes. "Thank you, sir, we will deliver your order in a couple of days," I heard the salesperson promise.

For the next 24 hours, I lie around in the salesperson's dark, smelly office bag. There were a few more orders like me in the bag, and lots of other papers. For company, we had a small box that contained the salesperson's lunch.

Next morning, the salesperson took me to the company's branch office and handed me and my friends over to a stern-looking lady at a desk with reading glasses at the tip of her nose. She examined me from top to bottom through her glasses. The scrutiny lasted less than 10 minutes (felt like an hour, though). She called the salesperson and handed me back to him. "There's a mandatory requirement missing. How many times do I have to tell you that we can not accept orders without this document? I'm afraid you will have to go right back to the customer and get it." The salesperson tried to convince her to keep me and promised he would get the document the next day, but she was firm. "I'm sorry, it's against company policy to accept incomplete orders. Besides, my time starts the moment I accept the order from you and enter it into the system—and I can't let your incomplete order make my performance chart look bad."

So, back I went into the dark bag. This time, I stayed there for 48 hours. The customer lived on the other side of town, and the salesperson did not want to go all the way there just for one order. He waited a couple of days until some other work took him to that part of town. Two days later, he had collected the required document from the customer, attached it to me, and took me back to the branch office.

The stern lady again examined me and the attached document. This time, she couldn't find any reason to reject me.

She entered some of the information that was written on me into her computer. All of this took 15 minutes.

After that, she put me in a tray, on top of several orders like me. I stayed there for several hours, during which more orders were piled on top of me one by one until I almost choked. At last, somebody put all the orders from the tray into a packet and shipped us off to the company's back office. All branch offices sent the orders they had collected to this back office for processing. It was now nearly 24 hours from the time the branch office had accepted me.

At the back office, a bunch of chirpy young people took me and the other orders out of our packets and subjected us to the same kind of scrutiny that the branch lady had. Only, these people were not so stern. When my turn came, after a 10-minute examination, I was thrown into a red basket labeled "reject." "Now what?" I thought to myself. My question was answered almost instantly when I heard the examiner telling her colleague, "This one has a signature missing. Can't these branch people ever do their jobs right the first time?" By the end of the day, the red basket was full of rejected orders like me. Some had signatures missing, some were not completely filled in, and some had mandatory documents missing. These had somehow escaped the scrutiny at the branch office, but got caught at the back office. The next day, I was sent back to the branch office in a packet. It had taken 72 hours from the time I was scrutinized at the back office until I reached the branch office again.

The stern lady called the salesperson on the phone. He came the next day to pick me up from the branch. The following day, he took me back to the customer for the missing signature. The customer seemed quite upset. He told off the salesperson, "My friend, you promised me delivery in two days. It's now nearly 10 days, and you haven't even started processing my order! You came back once for the missing document, and now for more signatures! Doesn't your company train you people to do your job right the first time?" The salesperson made a sheepish apology and promised to get the order processed without further delay.

Back at the branch, I went through the now-familiar routine once again. Fifteen minutes for scrutiny by the stern one and some data entered into her computer. I waited at the branch office for 24 hours before reaching the back office again, and another 12 hours in an in-tray at the back office before being taken up again for processing. This time, to my relief, I passed the scrutiny at the back office. It took 30 minutes to have the final product ready to be sent to the customer.

The rest of the story will be told by the final product.

I am the final product (I could be the product or service that customers buy from your company). I am told that it took just a few minutes to actually create me, but my dad (the sales order) had to go through a lot of back and forth before they could start creating me. My earliest memory after I was created is of sitting in the dispatch room along with several others like me. After we had sat there for a day, I was shipped to the customer. After spending three days in transport, I finally reached the customer. It had taken a full two weeks from the time the customer had first placed the order—and the salesperson had promised the customer that they would have me in two days!

But wait a minute—the total time that someone actually worked on me or on the sales order adds up to a mere two hours! Nevertheless, the customer had to wait for two weeks!

## IS THIS VALUE?

Welcome back from the autobiography. The same incident is described in a step-by-step table in Figure 15. Do such things happen occasionally in your company? While this may be an extreme example, in companies I have seen, such stories are by no means unheard of.

Now, coming back to the question of "what is value," pretend for a moment that you are the customer in this story (remember, it's your money that's paying for every single step in the process, including all the waste, such as avoidable rework and waiting). Assume further that the company actually allows you, the customer, to see what happens with your order inside the company, like a restaurant that allows customers to come into their kitchen and see how their order is prepared. And finally, assume that the company gives you the option of paying only for those steps in the process that you wish to pay for.

Did you notice that the time that the customer's requirement is actually being worked on is in minutes, while much of the time *wasted* on "waiting" or avoidable "transport" is in hours or days?

| Activity | Time |
|---|---|
| 1. Salesperson meets customer; customer writes application and hands over to salesperson | 30 mins |
| 2. Application lying with salesperson before being brought to branch office (Waiting) | 24 hrs |
| 3. Scrutiny at branch office | 10 mins |
| 4. Mandatory requirement missing—handed back to salesperson—salesperson goes back to customer and gets additional requirement (Defect/rework + Transport + Waiting) | 48 hrs |
| 5. Scrutiny and partial data entry at branch (partial Rework) | 15 mins |
| 6. Application waits at branch office to be dispatched to back office in a batch (Waiting) | 24 hrs |
| 7. Scrutiny at back office | 10 mins |
| 8. Mandatory requirement missing—sent back to branch (Defect/rework + Transport + Waiting) | 72 hrs |
| 9. Branch informs salesperson—time taken for salesperson to come to branch to collect (Waiting) | 24 hrs |
| 10. Salesperson goes back to customer and gets additional requirement (Rework + Transport + Waiting) | 24 hrs |
| 11. Scrutiny and partial data entry at branch (Rework) | 15 mins |
| 12. Application waits at branch to be dispatched to back office in a batch (Waiting) | 24 hrs |
| 13. Waiting at back office for further processing (Waiting) | 12 hrs |
| 14. Scrutiny and full data entry at back office; creation of end product (partial Rework) | 30 mins |
| 15. End product waiting for dispatch at back office (Waiting) | 24 hrs |
| 16. Dispatch desk hands over to courier for dispatch | 10 mins |
| 17. Time taken for delivery to customer (Transport) | 72 hrs |
| **Total time taken** | **350 hrs** |
| **Total non-value-added time** | **348 hrs** |
| **Total value-added time is two hours out of a total process time of 14 days!** | **2 hrs** |

**Figure 15** Value stream mapping story.

Chances are that you would be willing to pay for only the steps shown in the white boxes in Figure 15 (some customers may even question a few of these, especially the ones that are partial rework). The white boxes are the steps where somebody is actually working on the customer's requirement. The rest of the time and the remaining steps, from the customer's point of view, is pure waste. This brings out two important points that, in my opinion, must be remembered by everyone in every business or other organization that has customers. First, value can *only* be defined by the customer. Second, value is what the customer is willing to *pay* for.

> **Value can only *be defined by the customer.* Second, value is what the customer is willing to pay for.**

Seen this way, clearly, a major part of what we see in Figure 15 is non-value-adding. Only two hours out of 350 hours is value-adding! Non-value-adding time in excess of 90% of the total time is not uncommon. That said, we have to grant that perhaps not all of the non-value-adding time can be eliminated. For example, in some processes, certain steps may be non-value-adding from the customer's perspective, but may be required by regulatory or risk management or other requirements.

So, don't expect the 348 hours of non-value-adding time to come down to zero. But can we begin by knocking off, say, 20% or 30% of this non-value-adding time? Now, that sounds reasonable enough, doesn't it? We could knock off that much and then come back and see if we could reduce it some more.

Over the years, I have had the opportunity to see business after business do precisely this in process after process with amazing results. Some examples are given a little later in this chapter.

## THE INVISIBLE MOUNTAIN

I call this 348 hours of non-value-adding time the Invisible Mountain. It had been right there in front of us, staring at us all these years, and yet we had missed it! On the other hand, we had been (mostly in vain, and often at the cost of much pain and frustration to our people) foolishly attacking the two hours of value-adding work—to see if we could reduce a minute here or a few seconds there! Mostly, we just ended up (unnecessarily, as we now realize) stretching our systems and making our people bend backward to do what was impossible, and in any case not sustainable.

Sounds familiar? Why is this? Why did we try to attack and reduce the two hours of value-adding time when there was this mountain of 348 hours of non-value-adding time waiting to be reduced? The answer is simple. At that time, the two hours was all that was *visible* to us. The mountain of waste, as I said earlier, was invisible.

## VALUE STREAM MAPPING MAKES THE MOUNTAIN OF WASTE VISIBLE

The mountain of non-value-adding steps and time became visible only because somebody looked at the process the way it is shown in Figure 15. A few of us followed the sales order that was being worked on (or mostly, *not* worked on) all the way from the moment the customer handed it over the first time to the salesperson until the customer finally got what they had ordered. We shadowed that one order—almost *became* that order (remember the autobiography?)—and made a note of *everything* that happened to the application, including time spent in waiting. In place of the sales order, you can think of a part being produced in your factory, or any other process that happens in your business, irrespective of what business you are in.

What we did was to go to the place where the work happens, or *gemba*, as the Japanese call it, and walk the process as it actually happens. Only when you walk your process where it happens and see what happens with your own eyes will you be able to see your process as depicted in Figure 15.

If you are able to understand and appreciate what is shown in Figure 15, you have understood value stream mapping. For senior management and most managers, an understanding of this simple, yet hugely effective method of depicting your processes is enough to equip you to apply it and derive substantial business results. Students of Lean who wish to study more-detailed and technical aspects of value stream mapping may refer to any good text or paper on the subject.

You may have noticed some words in brackets to the right of several of the activities in Figure 15. I am sure you have guessed it already—these are different types of waste. They had always been there, right in front of us, yet invisible to us. Now that we had walked the process as it happened and mapped it as shown in Figure 15, these wastes suddenly became visible.

Once the mountain of waste became visible, we also started realizing how much it was costing the company directly and indirectly—though we may never know the full extent of this cost. In the example in Figure 15, total value-adding time is two hours out of a total time of two weeks. The remaining (non-value-adding) time means extra cost—of rework, or of avoidable communication or transport. Some of the customers who experience situations like this complain. Handling these complaints has a cost. And who knows how many customers just walked out on us due to such incidents? Surely, some of them would have told others about their bad experience—scaring potential customers away from us. And I haven't even started talking about other opportunity costs, for example, the salesperson could have closed another sale in the time they spent on rework, the branch and back office spent time on the same application two or three times, and customer call center agents could have been handling sales leads in the time taken to answer complaints.

The later in the process that errors are detected, the higher the cost of rework. Conversely, if the job is done right the first time, there would be zero cost of rework. In one company, we estimated that if rework happened in just 5% of the transactions, the cost (of rework) would be half a million dollars every year!

> *The later in the process that errors are detected, the higher the cost of rework. Conversely, if the job is done right the first time, there would be zero cost of rework. In one company, we estimated that if rework happened in just 5% of the transactions, the cost (of rework) would be half a million dollars every year!*

## YOU HAVE STARTED WINNING THE BATTLE AGAINST QUALITY PROBLEMS AND WASTE

We have spent considerable space on "making quality problems visible" in the last chapter and, so far, in this chapter, too. From years of experience, I am totally convinced that the bigger challenges to solving quality problems are, first, for senior management to be genuinely serious about continuous improvement, and, second, to have a culture and methods to make quality problems visible. If you have these two (remember, we haven't yet solved the quality problems—we just have an *intent* to do so, and have made the problems visible), trust me, you have won three-fourths of the battle. In most cases, the solutions suggested themselves the moment we made quality problems visible and got to the root cause of the problem (the story of root cause analysis is told in a later chapter).

## EXAMPLES OF FIGHTING WASTE AND RESULTS

Some examples of how quality problems or waste identified in Figure 15 were eliminated, and with what results, are given below.

In several businesses, we were able to reduce the waste due to defects and rework by beginning to measure and focus on people doing their jobs right the first time, or *first time right* (FTR). People were trained on FTR. Wherever possible, we introduced *poka-yoke*, or mistake-proofing, to help people do their jobs right the first time. We started linking a portion of salespeople's remuneration to FTR sales (sales orders submitted by them that were accurate and complete the first time and needed zero rework), and not merely the total business they brought in. CEOs and senior management started reviewing FTR performance. All this resulted in dramatic improvement in FTR. One company was able to increase the percentage of FTR sales orders from a mere 16% to 97%, and another company from 65% to 90%. This resulted in higher profits (by reducing the cost of rework), as well as higher customer satisfaction as orders were fulfilled on time.

At several stages in the autobiography, the order had to wait for up to 24 hours for a batch to accumulate before they were picked up for processing. Often, batch processing is the cause of the waste of *waiting*. Moving away from batch processing to continuous processing (or as close to continuous as possible, as it may sometimes not be practical to move to pure continuous processing, ideal though it may be) can significantly reduce waiting. One company was able to double their productivity by increasing the frequency of picking up sales orders for processing from once every 24 hours to once every 30 minutes. The number of orders they were able to process every hour (with the same number of people) went up from 113 to 219. What they had done was *heijunka*, or leveling the workload.

Multiskilling of employees through on-the-job training also helps to level the workload. For example, at one company, sales orders from across the country were received at a common back office for processing. The first step at the back office was to enter each order received in a spreadsheet register. This was done by an employee who was trained to do only this step. This took just a few seconds per order. This employee would check the in-tray about once every two hours, enter orders that had arrived into the spreadsheet, and pass them on for the next step. The second step was to scrutinize the order to make sure it was complete and error-free. This was done by a second employee, who took about two minutes per order. The third step was to enter the order into the company's core system, which would cause the order to get processed. This step was done by a third employee, and it took about 10 minutes per order. Often, the employee responsible for step 1 would have no work, while the third employee would have orders piled up awaiting entry into the core system. However, on days when the first employee couldn't come to work, all orders would lie in the in-tray until the next day. The second and third employees would also remain idle that day. Once Lean was introduced, the company trained all three employees on all three steps. Orders coming in were assigned to them by rotation, and the person getting an order was responsible for all three steps. This not only significantly leveled the work, but led to a remarkable increase in productivity (there was a sharp increase in the number of orders that could be processed in a day by the same three employees). The employees also reported that they found their job more satisfying than before.

Another business achieved a 13% increase in productivity by simply rearranging the workstations of employees according to the flow of the process. The rearrangement resulted in reduced *motion* of people and *transport* of material. This opportunity was identified during a process walk at the gemba.

One company used a special type of packaging for its products for "premium" customers whose purchase value exceeded a certain level. For other customers, the product was packed in ordinary packaging. The product's quality and delivery time were exactly the same for all customers. The special packaging cost five times the ordinary one. I once had an opportunity to meet some of the premium customers. I asked them what they thought about the special packaging, expecting them to appreciate the company's gesture. However, their response surprised me and others in the company. Most of the premium customers said they attached little value to the special packaging. Some customers even thought that this was a gimmick. "Give us a good quality product, on time, and at the right price," was their near-unanimous message to the company. We realized again that this *extra processing* was a waste. And we had thought all along that our premium customers would be happy with it. The company decided to stop the special packaging, and, instead, focus on good quality and on-time delivery to customers. With the money saved by discontinuing the special packaging, the company was able to give customers a slightly better price compared to the competition, as well as increase their profit a bit. This experience also taught us that the easiest and best way (actually, the *only* way) of learning what is value to the customer is, well, to just go out and *ask* the customer. This may sound simple enough, but more than a few times I have seen people inside the company trying to guess what is important to the customer and leading the company to make expensive mistakes, like the one in this example.

In another company, certain process steps that were done because they had "always" been done (for years) were questioned and even eliminated once it became clear that they neither added value from the customer's perspective nor served any other purpose. Again, the wasteful steps became visible only when we walked the process as it actually happened on the ground and mapped it as shown in Figure 15.

## LEAN CAN DOUBLE YOUR PROFITS

One group of large companies achieved 65 million dollars of direct contribution to their profit by way of cost savings from Lean over a five-year period. In fact, when these businesses were hit by the global recession of 2008, Lean turned out to be their biggest savior. In that difficult time, revenues just would not come, and the only option many companies had to try and protect their profits was to look at how they could save costs. And they found their answer in Lean and its methodical way of identifying and reducing waste. In that difficult year, Lean was the biggest contributor to profits, and these companies were able to weather the storm better than many of their competitors. And the good news is that when times got better and business volumes started increasing again, so did their savings. They then realized that the productivity improvements and waste reduction that they built into their process during the recession was giving them sustained, even bigger, benefits when business came back.

How was this? It shouldn't surprise anybody because, unlike the desperate and mindless "cost cutting" that companies sometimes resort to in difficult times (such as laying off skilled employees), which only comes back to hurt the company when times get better, Lean is about identifying and eliminating *waste*. In Lean, cost savings are a result of cutting waste. This kind of cost saving will not hurt you in the future—in fact, the benefits tend to be sustained year after year.

> *In Lean, cost savings are a result of cutting waste. This kind of cost saving will not hurt you in the future—in fact, the benefits tend to be sustained year after year.*

For example, one large company (triggered by the recession) realized that a large portion of their fairly substantial spending on marketing material and brochures was just wasted. The stuff used to lie around in branch offices or with salespeople, and never even reach customers. Unfortunately, the company had no way of telling just which portion would get wasted. When Lean was introduced, it helped them identify this waste (it's called *inventory*). A "pull"-based inventory management system was introduced, which helped to make branch offices and salespeople accountable for the material they took. Using the new system, the company would replenish the material "just-in-time," so that the branch office didn't need to stock piles of these supplies any more. Just this one initiative of reducing waste in marketing material saved the company an estimated six million dollars in a bad year! And since the improvement is permanent, the savings continue year after year. In fact, we found that the savings are even higher in good years because the overall volumes are higher (if we had not made this process Lean, the waste on the higher volumes in a good year would have increased proportionately).

## IS THIS RELEVANT IN SERVICE INDUSTRIES?

Thanks to the example set by companies like Toyota, the world today knows about Lean. Most of the examples of Lean that we hear or read about tend to be from manufacturing. Perhaps because of this, some managers and business leaders seem to mistakenly think that Lean principles are relevant only in manufacturing.

Our experience in various service companies shows that nothing could be farther from the truth. As a matter of fact, several of the examples of successful implementation and results given in this chapter are from service companies. If anything, Lean and other quality principles are even more important for many service companies than for manufacturing. This is because waste in a service setup can be even more dangerous as it is often less obvious than in manufacturing, though it may be costing the company heavily. I have seen every single one of the nine types of waste in service companies, too. And I have also seen them successfully apply the Toyota principles and value stream mapping to reduce them.

> *If anything, Lean and other quality principles are even more important for many service companies than for manufacturing. This is because waste in a service setup can be even more dangerous as it is often less obvious than in manufacturing, though it may be costing the company heavily.*

After years of helping companies fight waste, I am convinced about the near-universal applicability and relevance of the Toyota Production System and Lean.

## INVOLVING PARTNERS

We found much truth in Toyota's belief in involving partners and suppliers. In fact, in quite a few businesses that I worked with (I believe this is true with many companies in today's world) we found such a significant proportion of the work being done by distributors and outsourced partners that, to achieve any meaningful improvement that could be felt by our customers, we had no choice but to involve our partners in our Lean journey. We found that it is important to involve people who are part of the process that is to be made Lean—whether they are direct employees or partners is irrelevant.

## NOW THAT YOU CAN SEE THE MOUNTAIN, DEMOLISH IT!

As you may have noticed from the last chapter and much of this chapter, Lean seems to attach a lot of importance to making quality problems visible. To me, Lean seems to be largely about making quality problems and the mountain of waste visible. The assumption (and in our experience, it is a fair assumption) is that once the problems are visible, the solutions will become apparent.

This chapter talked about some techniques and examples of solving quality problems or reducing waste permanently, such as *heijunka* (leveling), just-in-time, *poka-yoke* (mistake-proofing), first time right, multiskilling, designing the workplace as per the flow of the process, pull, inventory management, and discontinuing extra processing.

In fact, the benefits of doing our jobs right the first time—especially salespeople getting sales orders right the first time (because in most companies, this is the starting point in the entire value chain of the company)—proved to be so huge that the entire next chapter is about first time right (FTR).

# 9

# Double Your Revenue and Profits without Selling More: The Importance of First Time Right

> *You don't get ahead by making products and then separating the good from the bad, because that's wasteful.*
>
> —W. Edwards Deming

First time right (FTR), or doing things right the first time, is an important concept in quality. Some experts go to the extent of calling "first time right" the very definition of quality.

*Poka-yoke*, or mistake-proofing (using automation wherever possible), plays an important role in helping people do their jobs right the first time. However, we learned that it is equally important to *intend* and *strive* to do things right the first time—what I call having the FTR *attitude*.

> **Poka-yoke, or mistake-proofing (using automation wherever possible), plays an important role in helping people do their jobs right the first time. However, we learned that it is equally important to intend and strive to do things right the first time—what I call having the FTR attitude.**

## WHY IS FTR SO IMPORTANT?

It is a truism that we all need to do our jobs right the first time, but I didn't realize just how damaging or wasteful *not* doing so can be.

Consider this example. A tailoring shop received an order to make 100 dresses. Assume that the dressmaking process involves only three steps—measuring, cutting, and stitching. The shop has three employees—one person does each step. Each employee does their job right 90% of the time, the remaining 10% is waste. Most of us think that if we do our jobs right 90% of the time, we're doing a pretty good job, right? So, to make the 100 dresses, I thought they would need to buy 10% extra cloth to allow for this waste. How wrong I was!

Assume the shop purchased exactly enough material for 100 dresses. The employee responsible for the first step does a correct job of measuring and marking the material (for cutting) for 90 dresses. The remaining 10 are incorrectly measured and marked.

The employee responsible for the second step (cutting) has thus received correctly measured and marked material for only 90 dresses. The remaining 10 are going to be cut wrong anyway, because they are wrongly measured and marked in the first place (the input itself is defective). This employee cuts 90% of the 90 good pieces correctly—resulting in 81 correctly cut pieces.

The third employee thus receives 81 defect-free cut pieces for stitching. She does her job right 90% of the time—resulting in about 73 correctly stitched dresses.

So, material for 100 dresses has resulted in 73 good dresses. With everybody doing their jobs right 90% of the time, the waste is not 10% but a whopping 27%!

Who's going to pay for this 27% wasted material? The customer who ordered the dresses? Or the tailoring shop?

If you'd like a bit of jargon, the *first pass yield*, also known as *throughput yield*, of each individual step is 90%. However, the *rolled throughput yield* of the entire process is only 73% (90% × 90% × 90% = about 73%). To keep the example simple, we have not considered that some of the defective work might have been rectified subsequently through rework. On the other hand, this rework could require additional time and material costs, which have also not been considered in the example. It is not necessary to complicate the example with all these, because the message is going to remain the same, and the message is this:

> Every one of your people doing their jobs right 90% of the time is *not* going to give you 90% defect-free output. The defect percentage is going to be much, much higher than 10%.

And I'd be surprised if your customer is willing to pay for this waste. Can the tailoring shop that delivered 73 defect-free dresses make their customer pay for 100 dresses? Would this customer ever come back to this tailor? The answers are obvious.

> *Every one of your people doing their jobs right 90% of the time is not going to give you 90% defect-free output. The defect percentage is going to be much, much higher than 10%.*

And, I hope, this story makes the importance of FTR, or everybody doing their job right the first time, obvious. We realized that FTR is relevant in *any* job or function—even in selling. That story is next.

## FTR IN SALES

Much has been written about the obvious need for FTR given its importance in improving efficiency and reducing waste and costs associated with rework. Many examples of FTR that one comes across pertain to operations or customer service, for example, resolving a customer's query right the first time. However, I didn't come across too many examples of *selling* right the first time, that is, FTR in sales. Also, I didn't come across too many published examples where the business benefits of FTR have been measured. On the other hand, *not* selling right the first time (this could include errors or omissions as in the "autobiography of the sales order" in the last chapter, or intentional *mis*-selling or false promises by the salesperson) could have fairly serious consequences, as we learned.

Implementing the concept of first time right in sales led to spectacular results, not merely in increasing the quality of sales, reducing cost of rework, and increasing customer satisfaction, but in revenue and profits.

I believe our experience could be replicated in almost any business. Hence, I thought it might be useful to share the results of our experiments—if one may call them that—with promoting FTR in sales. We also decided to measure and see if FTR actually helps, where, and how much.

In some businesses that I had an opportunity to work with, one of the areas where we particularly concentrated our FTR improvement efforts was to try and ensure that our salespeople brought in sales orders that were complete and accurate the first time—not requiring any rework. This was for several reasons. We found that sales orders that were not right the first time caused delays in the customer finally getting what they ordered, customer dissatisfaction, delays and rework in the company's own internal processes, and avoidable cost of rework.

As the sales order is the trigger or starting point of a whole chain of events, an order that is not right the first time delays the entire process down the line. The sales order is the first experience with the company for many customers, and it is important for the first experience to be a good one. Our experience was that a sales order that was not FTR would, at best, lead to a delay in delivering the customer's order, or worse, lead to the customer getting the wrong quantity or a different product than what they wanted, or worst, cause the customer to cancel their order or stop future business. A wrong sales order could also cause the wrong product to be made and shipped, and avoidable costs of correcting and reshipping, not to mention the cost of handling complaints.

At our group of businesses, we were convinced about the usefulness of FTR and tried to promote it wherever possible. However, when we started measuring the difference between selling right the first time and *not* selling right the first time, the numbers were astounding and proved to us that FTR is one of the most important business measures for a CEO to personally focus on. In this chapter, we will look at two real-life examples of the impact of FTR in sales on five very different, and equally important, outcomes.

## WHAT IS AN FTR SALE?

FTR in sales is simply ensuring that during the sale, the company (including salespeople, distributors, or agents who sell on behalf of the company) collects 100 percent complete and accurate requirements from the customer the first time, and that the customer is not pestered again and again because the company failed to collect or understand some requirement completely or accurately. These requirements could include the order form or screen, supporting documents, the customer's payment, or customer specifications. It also includes providing complete and accurate information required to be given to the customer "first time right" so that there are no surprises later. Often, the company needs to go back to the customer a second or third time because they failed to either provide or collect some information, document, or other requirement the first time. The second, and more obvious, part of an FTR sale is making sure that the company delivers the customer's requirement accurately the first time, on time, and without any rework. It goes without saying that any sale where false promises are made to the customer automatically qualifies as "*non*-FTR."

## WHERE IS FTR SELLING RELEVANT?

Our experiments were mostly conducted in large service companies such as insurance, investments, lending, other financial services, and telecom. These are industries where the company typically has to both provide information to and collect information and specifications from the customer before each sale (often in the form of a sales order and related documents). However, it seems logical that the concept of FTR in sales and its benefits would be equally relevant in almost any manufacturing or service business. After all, which customer in *any* industry would like to put up with a "not right the first time" experience? Even if some customers complete the purchase despite a non-FTR experience, what kind of first impression are they going to carry, and will they come back to such a company for a repeat purchase?

> *Which customer in any industry would like to put up with a "not right the first time" experience?*

## FTR AND COST OF REWORK

First, let's look at the more obvious linkages. It seemed quite obvious that FTR would contribute to lower cost of rework and higher customer satisfaction.

The savings through reduced cost of rework were the most obvious and straightforward to measure. Every time a salesperson submitted a sales order that was not right the first time, it resulted in the salesperson (or worse, someone else from the company) traveling back to the customer for more information or corrections, documents flowing back and forth, communication expenses, operations staff spending double or more company-paid time on processing the sale as compared to an FTR order, and so forth. Obviously, all this is wasteful activity that no customer would be willing to pay for. When this was measured, one company realized that non-FTR sales were adding 20% to the cost of processing on account of rework, directly eating into the company's profits.

## FTR AND CUSTOMER SATISFACTION

Common sense also suggested that customers who have a first time right purchase experience would be happier than customers who are bothered several times by the company for the same purchase. One company decided to measure how much happier the FTR customers were. Fortunately, for the last several years, the company had commissioned a globally reputed research firm to do an annual independent survey of customer satisfaction. This year, they asked the research firm to measure the satisfaction score separately for customers who had experienced an FTR sale and those who hadn't (other things being equal). Customers who had experienced an FTR sale rated their overall satisfaction (not merely on the purchase experience, but overall satisfaction with the company) a full 10 points higher (on a scale of 100) than customers who didn't experience an FTR sale. According to the research firm's global norms, the score is in the "excellent" range for FTR customers, while it is in the "average" range for non-FTR customers. The research firm's experts pointed out that the 10 points difference represents a statistically very significant difference in overall satisfaction levels with the company for the two groups of customers.

In both examples above, we had always suspected that FTR sales would have some impact on cost of rework and customer satisfaction. However, most people in the company admitted that the enormity of this impact came as a revelation to them.

## FTR AND COMPANY IMAGE

Another serious impact, though not so easy to measure, was on the company's image. Going by the oft-repeated fact that a dissatisfied customer is more likely to tell their friends about their bad experience than a happy customer is to talk about their good experience, clearly, the company's brand image was taking a beating with each non-FTR sales order.

## THE IMPACT OF FTR ON REVENUE, PROFITS, AND SALES PRODUCTIVITY

Another outcome of non-FTR sales that is often overlooked by companies (perhaps because they have never measured it and hence are unaware of what they are losing) is lost business or lost revenue. One company noticed that only about 20% of the sales orders submitted by its salespeople were FTR. In other words, in 80% of the sales orders, the company had to go back to the customer more than once to complete some requirement that was missed the first time. What was really worrisome to the company was that nearly half of this 80% of customers had changed their mind when they went back to them, and were no longer interested in buying.

The reasons for the customers having changed their mind were several—some of them had found a better deal with a competitor, some did not need the product any longer, while some customers bluntly said that their first impression was that here was a company who couldn't do their job right the first time, and they didn't want to deal with such a company.

While the reasons were several, the impact on the company was serious—lost business or lost revenue. Its revenue was about 40% lower than what it could have been if only its salespeople did their jobs right the first time (with the same number of sales orders from the same number of customers, mind you). In the CEO's words, "this was money almost in our hands, which we were unable to hold on to."

The company realized that it was running after sourcing more customers and more sales orders, only to put them into a leaking bucket, where a large percentage of them would not result in revenue to the company. They decided to do something about it. As the CEO put it, "What's the point in running after more customers and more sales orders if most of them don't result in revenue? Instead, can we first figure out a way to convert a much larger proportion of the 'nearly-done' deals we have on hand to 'done' deals?" They introduced a serious training program on FTR for all their salespeople, from the most senior levels to the "feet on the street" employees. They also trained distributors and agents. A significant part of salespeople's and distributors' performance appraisals and incentives was linked to FTR sales and not merely total sales.

In a few months, the company's efforts started paying off. The percentage of FTR orders to total sales orders sourced went from 20% to over 90%! A year later, the CEO acknowledged that their revenue for the year was 35% higher than it otherwise would have been, solely because of the increase in FTR sales. The impact on profit was even more spectacular. The company estimated that its profit for the year was about 50% higher than it otherwise would have been, given that an overwhelming majority of sales orders were now FTR. Compare this to the situation a year earlier, when 80% of the orders were incorrect or incomplete, calling for additional cost of rework. And even after incurring this cost, half of the non-FTR orders never got converted into actual sales.

The additional revenue and profits were achieved with the same number of customers and sales orders, at no additional cost and no additional sales effort (in fact, with significantly less effort, as the effort that was earlier spent on rework was now almost entirely eliminated).

Over a period of time, the increasing FTR also led to dramatic improvement in sales productivity, that is, the number of sales successfully closed per salesperson or per distributor each week. This was logical, because all the time that was previously spent on rework and multiple trips or calls to the customer to correct and complete the same incorrect or incomplete sales order was now freed up for new FTR sales.

We believe that the impact of FTR on morale of employees and distributors is also positive. Seeing their sales numbers grow with every unit of effort is always more satisfying to a salesperson than spending time and effort on rework.

## MENTAL BLOCKS

We experienced that the most difficult part was not defining FTR or measuring it, but overcoming the mental blocks that got in the way. A large company with nearly nine million customers decided to measure the impact of FTR in sales. Everybody made the right noises in meetings that FTR was important and should be measured. However, when we tried to actually measure FTR and make salespeople accountable for it, it became obvious that some of the seniors, whose involvement was vital, were not serious. These were people with over 20 years of selling experience in the industry. They had worked with several large industry players, including the market leader. In their decades of selling, they had never heard of the concept of FTR in sales, let alone it being measured and them being made accountable for it.

It took months of dogged persuasion. However, I suspect what really convinced the skeptics were the results. Who doesn't like more results (and bonuses) without more effort (actually with less effort)? As with many other things in life, perhaps, most of us really get convinced only when we measure and see the results for ourselves.

## LESSON LEARNED—ONLY SALES MUST BE RESPONSIBLE FOR FTR IN SALES

During our experimental phase, we learned an important lesson. I am sharing it here so you don't have to learn it the hard way, as we did. Some of us tried to take a shortcut. In many companies, there is a mentality that Sales is a "sacred cow" that must not be bothered by mundane things (such as FTR), and this company was no exception. Instead of "burdening" Sales with the task of doing their jobs right the first time, one company let Sales continue to bring in a high proportion of junk (read incorrect and incomplete orders), and put an army of operations staff to work separating the good from the bad. The operations staff were also responsible to go back to the customers to get missing documents or information.

After wasting a few months with this arrangement, the company realized that neither FTR nor revenue were increasing. Customers were angrier than before because now they had to deal with different people from the company for the same purchase. These people didn't seem to talk to each other, and often the customer had to repeat the same story separately to different people. Naturally, many customers started taking their business elsewhere.

The company realized that they were only fooling themselves. They learned the important lesson that to be "first time right," a job must be done right the first time by the person whose job it is in the first place. Otherwise, it is not FTR. Separating the good from the bad, whether it is done by Sales or Operations is not FTR. They realized that there is no option but for Sales to take ownership of sales and the customer. It was only after this realization dawned that the company started truly working toward FTR in sales.

## HOW DO YOU KNOW IF IT'S WORKING?

We learned (again the hard way) that FTR by itself is merely an enabler (though an important enabler) and not an end in itself. The moment the company started using FTR as a measure of salespeople's performance, the FTR numbers in some locations started shooting up suspiciously. Some of the numbers seemed too good to be true. On investigation, it was found that some of them were cooked to make the charts look good.

After this experience, the company, while continuing to retain FTR as one of the performance measures for sales, also started linking the input measure (for example, percentage of FTR sales orders) to one or more of the five measureable outcomes described in this chapter. The measurable outcomes of FTR in sales are reduced cost of rework, contribution to customer satisfaction, revenue, profits, and sales productivity. Once this linking was done, there was no incentive to cook the FTR percentage numbers because a salesperson reporting high FTR would also need to show its impact on one or more of these five outcomes. Gradually, salespeople realized that FTR was helping them and the company to achieve higher revenue, profits, and bonuses. This was when the true pursuit of FTR in sales began in the company.

## WHAT YOU CAN DO

If you are a CEO or business leader, remember that the company often pays for sales efforts irrespective of whether the sales efforts result in revenue or not. In the companies in the above examples, it was only when the CEO became serious about FTR in sales, and made their seriousness known, that others in the company became serious. Once convinced, the CEOs ensured that training, performance measurement, remuneration, and bonuses for salespeople at all levels, as well as for distributors, were tied to FTR. The FTR increase examples mentioned above were the result of structured, time-bound quality improvement projects sponsored by the CEO and championed by the company's sales head. We also learned through experience that FTR is not merely a measure, but a culture. An organization-wide culture that values everybody in every function doing their job right the first time can give huge edge over competition. And only the business leader can build this culture.

If you are the quality leader, this could be your next big project— an exciting opportunity to bring huge value to the business. In the examples above, it was the quality leader who initially helped the business define and measure FTR, acted as a culture change agent to make the organization serious about it, and facilitated the FTR improvement project. The project was run as a pilot in a few selected locations to begin with. After seeing the results of the pilot, it was spread to all locations across the company.

So, irrespective of what business you are in, start measuring FTR, make your sales leaders accountable for it, and see the results.

> **Irrespective of what business you are in, start measuring FTR, make your sales leaders accountable for it, and see the results.**

In this chapter and the previous one, we saw some techniques and examples of solving quality problems or reducing waste permanently, such as *heijunka* (leveling), just-in-time, *poka-yoke* (mistake-proofing), first time right, multiskilling, designing the workplace as per the flow of the process, pull, inventory management, and discontinuing extra processing.

In the next chapter, we will look at the structured problem-solving approach of Six Sigma.

# 10
# A Management Philosophy Called Six Sigma

*Once you understand that "variation is evil,"
you're 60 percent of the way to becoming a Six
Sigma expert.*

—Jack Welch

A CEO with whom I once worked remarked, after his business achieved some remarkable successes with Six Sigma projects, "Why, this is the way I am going to manage this company from now on. You can call it Six Sigma or any other name you like."

As Jack Welch (2005) puts it, "Six Sigma is a quality program that improves your customers' experience, lowers your costs, and builds better leaders. Six Sigma accomplishes that by reducing waste and inefficiency."

That's the whole point of this chapter. Six Sigma, and, for that matter, Lean and other techniques, can actually be management philosophies for visionary business leaders, rather than mere sets of "tools."

First a word on what this chapter is *not*—it isn't a treatise on the Six Sigma tool set. The tools are undoubtedly important, but, in my experience, Six Sigma can be much more than a mere collection of statistical tools. I have had the satisfaction of working with companies and leaders who achieved significant and sustained business results by using the structured define–measure–analyze–improve–control (DMAIC) approach of Six Sigma (see Table 4) to solve business problems and also bring about an organizational

**Table 4**  The DMAIC problem-solving approach of Six Sigma.

| Project phase | What is done at this phase |
| --- | --- |
| **Define** (Define the problem and make the case for the project) | • Identify the customer and their needs<br>• Define the problem and goal<br>• Form project team<br>• Set milestones<br>• Create project charter |
| **Measure** (Measure the problem and identify what data are needed) | • Map as-is process<br>• Make data collection plan<br>• Begin data collection |
| **Analyze** (Analyze the data to identify the root cause of the problem and identify solutions) | • Listen to the voice of the process<br>• Select appropriate tools and analyze data<br>• Identify root causes of defects<br>• Identify wastes and reasons for them |
| **Improve** (Test and implement solution) | • Brainstorm solution<br>• Select solution, pilot, and test pilot results<br>• Implement solution |
| **Control** (Ensure that improvement is sustained) | • Validate potential failures<br>• Ensure that solutions are built into the process so that they will be sustained<br>• Monitor sustaining of improvement |

culture transformation from working on gut-feel to working based on data and analysis.

The certifications like Black Belts and Green Belts may add to the motivation that employees and teams derive from delivering quantified business results through their Six Sigma projects. And the good news is that you don't have to be a Six Sigma expert to derive spectacular and sustained business results from Six Sigma. From the experience of involvement in Lean and Six Sigma projects for a dozen years, I am convinced that the power of Six Sigma as a management philosophy comes simply because it brings structure, discipline, and focus to the business and business processes.

In our businesses, the DMAIC approach brought a structured, time-bound approach to solving problems, and fixing the issue rather than fixing the blame. The management reviews (of quality improvement projects) that Six Sigma forced us to do brought discipline and focus of management attention. The *control* phase at the end of every Six Sigma project made us ensure that the improvement was sustained and that the process was less volatile (that is, had less variation or sprung fewer surprises) than before.

No doubt, there are some excellent examples of Six Sigma projects—especially in manufacturing and engineering—that make effective use of higher-end statistical tools and design of experiments. I have had the opportunity to witness quite a few myself. Unfortunately, however (in my opinion), the hype around statistical tools and manufacturing examples has probably led some business leaders to believe either that Six Sigma is applicable only in manufacturing or that Six Sigma is all about high-end statistics, or both. The application of and real business results from Six Sigma could possibly be even more widespread than they are today if more business leaders would look upon Lean and Six Sigma as management philosophies in a broader and more strategic sense. I also believe it is the responsibility of quality professionals to help business leaders to see and use these as a strategic management philosophy.

> **The application of and real business results from Six Sigma could possibly be even more widespread than they are today if more business leaders would look upon Lean and Six Sigma as management philosophies in a broader and more strategic sense.**

I have had the gratification of working with several businesses and leaders from diverse industries that have adopted this broader outlook and derived all-round, long-term business benefits as a result. And an overwhelming majority of Six Sigma projects in companies that derived significant companywide benefit from Six Sigma required just the simplest of statistical tools. In fact, we found that the Six Sigma experts who are able to deliver the biggest business results are those who have a good grasp of the methodology and tools and, more importantly, the ability to select the most relevant few tools for each business problem (and, even more importantly, avoid wasting time on irrelevant tools).

I have a strong suspicion that business leaders around the world who have derived significant business results through Six Sigma are not necessarily expert statisticians, but they understand very well that volatility and unpredictable variation in how their processes behave is *bad* for their business. Welch (2005) says, "That's Six Sigma—the elimination of unpleasant surprises and broken promises . . . . Once you understand the simple maxim 'variation is evil,' you're 60 percent of the way to becoming a Six Sigma expert."

> *I have a strong suspicion that business leaders around the world who have derived significant business results through Six Sigma are not necessarily expert statisticians, but they understand very well that volatility and unpredictable variation in how their processes behave is bad for their business.*

These leaders also know how to select and focus on a few vital projects that are of strategic importance to the business. And they know how to review these projects. If you would like a few tips on how to review quality improvement projects in your company, see Figure 16. Figure 17 provides a template or questionnaire of

- During the CEO's review, only champions (senior leaders typically reporting to the CEO) must make the presentation. Champions in turn must review projects in their area more frequently and in more detail with their project team.
- Insist that review presentations show data—not English. Have a review template and enforce this. This will save the CEO time (see Figure 17 for CEO's quality project review template).
- Freeze and physically sign off on the project charter at the start of each project. Do not keep changing it. Sign off on any change. Refer to the charter at the beginning of the review.
- Do not allow project teams to jump to corrective action based on mere brainstorming or gut-feel—ask to see the data that support their recommendations.
- Do not allow manipulation of the definition of a "defect." (For example, reducing complaints by categorizing them as "requests.")
- During your project reviews, ensure that the *link* between the analysis and recommended corrective actions is evident.

**Figure 16** CEO's quality project review guidelines.

**Question 1:** Show your project charter. What is the problem statement, goal statement, and definition of defect as per your charter? Is the charter signed off?

**Question 2:** For the above problem statement, based on *data* you have collected and analyzed—and *not* based on mere brainstorming or gut-feel—what are the top few categories or main causes that account for about 80% of the problem? Show your data and analysis.

**Question 3:** For the above "top few" categories of defects—based on further analysis using data—what are the root causes you have identified? Show your data and analysis.

**Question 4:** Based on the above root causes, what corrective actions have you recommended?

**Question 5:** In the case of cost-saving/waste elimination projects, what types of waste and cost-saving opportunities have you identified? Are defects, rework, overconsumption, waiting time, non-value-adding process steps, and so on, causing waste? What corrective actions do you plan to implement to eliminate/minimize these wastes?

**Question 6:** What is the status of implementation of these corrective actions? What is the completion date for implementation of each corrective action?

**Question 7:** Due to the above corrective actions, what is the improvement in the performance measure on your project charter? Show actual results for the last three months.

**Question 8:** Is customer satisfaction one of the objectives of this project? If yes, identify which specific measure of customer satisfaction would be impacted by your project. Show the customer satisfaction scores on this measure before and after your project.

**Question 9:** Is there a direct financial benefit (revenue enhancement or cost savings) due to this project? Show your financial calculation and assumptions.

**Question 10:** Is your project on track as per the original timelines on the project charter? Do you face any roadblocks to successful completion of your project?

**Question 11:** Have you put in place a *permanent* measurement system or "dashboard" to enable measurement, monitoring, and reporting on this project's performance measure on a monthly basis? Before closing the project, have the project leader and champion used this measurement system to monitor performance for at least three months to ensure sustaining of results? Show the dashboard. Does the project champion take responsibility to continue to measure, monitor, and report performance on this measure each month even after project closure?

**Question 12:** Show the project completion report with project results and sign-offs.

Note: This guide is for the CEO's review. In addition, the champion must review projects regularly along with their project team. The champion's review must be more frequent and more detailed. A quality facilitator can provide support on selection of appropriate LSS tools at each phase of the project, their correct application by the project leader, proper data collection and analysis, and necessary process changes.

**Figure 17** CEO's quality project review template.

review questions that CEOs can use when they review quality improvement projects, in order to keep their reviews shorter and more effective.

Business leaders know that performance measures based purely on averages can be misleading because averages can mask defects that their customers experience. An example should make this clear. An airline has two scheduled flights. One takes off 30 minutes before its scheduled time, and the other 30 minutes late. If this airline measured their performance purely based on averages, they may happily think that, on average, their flights were on time. However, what their customers on both flights experienced is a defect. In all likelihood, this airline either corrected the way they measure their performance, or is no more (the airline, that is). Obviously, a better measure would be to look at the number or proportion of flights that took off (or did not take off) on time.

A seemingly silly example, and I am sure you don't have any such measures based on averages or means in your business that hide defects from you. We did—and learned our lessons the hard way. At one time, we had measures like *average* time to process customer orders and *average* time to resolve customer complaints. In most months, our performance used to look good (or so we thought). What we didn't realize was that some percentage of the orders or complaints were processed *ahead* of time, and some were *late*. Like the airline in the story, at the end of the month, the *average* performance looked good. However, in reality we had unhappy customers, in a whopping 20% of the cases, whose orders or complaints were processed late. We came to know about them only when they canceled their orders or stopped giving us business. When our Six Sigma program opened our eyes to this problem with averages, the measurement system was corrected to look at the number and proportion of defects (delayed orders or complaints, in this example). We now look at the proportion of delayed orders or complaints rather than the average. This way, even if there is only a single delayed case in the month, it doesn't escape attention. Six Sigma helped us to focus attention on unstable processes that were subject to variation or volatility in their behavior and output (this is just another type of quality problem that becomes visible when we correct our measurement system).

Once the problem (or symptom) became visible, the next step was to get to the root cause of the problem. In most projects, simple techniques like Pareto (80:20) and why–why analysis helped us to identify the root cause. Once the root cause is identified, the solution usually just suggests itself.

## THE PROJECT CHARTER, AND REPORTING RESULTS FROM LEAN SIX SIGMA (LSS)

Like many companies, we found the practice of signing off on a formal *project charter* (a document defining the scope of the project, the project leader and team, timelines, target, and so on) at the start of every quality improvement project to be very useful. A sample project charter template is shown in Figure 18. Similarly, a one-page *project completion report* showing the actual results of the project is also signed off at the end of the project. Typically, the CEO, project champion, and project leader sign off on the charter and the project completion report. For projects that have a direct financial benefit (revenue or cost savings), we followed a practice of having the chief financial officer verify the financial benefits.

In my experience, one of the biggest factors responsible for the sustaining of the LSS initiative is the fact that we made it mandatory for every business to measure and report the number of LSS projects completed every month and the quantified business results achieved through these projects. Project leaders and their teams, senior functional heads ("champions"), and even business leaders derive considerable motivation from seeing their LSS results grow month after month. The practice of monthly reporting made this possible. The simple discipline of measuring and reporting the results monthly (this has happened for years now) has been an important factor responsible for long-term continuity of the LSS program and its results.

## LEAN AND SIX SIGMA—A POWERFUL COMBINATION

Too much has been written about how the disciplines of Lean and Six Sigma can or can not work together—with equally compelling arguments on both sides. Without taking sides in this debate, I would just like to share that our actual experience implementing these two as a combination in business after business has been extremely positive. We found that Lean principles, when combined with the data and analysis-based problem-solving rigor of Six Sigma and the DMAIC project approach, present a powerful combination that gave our businesses significant and sustained results.

They also present a valuable professional learning and growth opportunity to employees in any field. Many employees reported

**116** Chapter Ten

| Project title: | | |
|---|---|---|
| Project team | Business impact | Critical milestones |
| CEO (sponsor): | ☐ Revenue enhancement | Project start date: |
| Champion: | ☐ Cost optimization | Project end date: |
| Project leader: | ☐ Customer responsiveness | **Definition of opportunity** |
| Quality facilitator: | ☐ Customer/intermediary satisfaction | |
| Team members: | ☐ Others (please specify) | **Definition of defect:** |
| | Financial impact (to be signed off by CFO) | |
| Business case | Problem statement: | |
| | Goal statement: | |
| | Critical to quality (CTQ) measure | Baseline | Target |
| In scope | Out of scope | | |

**Figure 18** Sample project charter (blank template).

that the experience of leading or working on a Lean Six Sigma team for one or two projects permanently changed their way of thinking and working. Even when they are not on a formal project, they are more waste-conscious, structured, analytical, comfortable working with data, and result oriented. When this behavioral transformation happens to more and more employees, it leads to organization-wide culture transformation. I have myself witnessed this transformation in several organizations.

We saw earlier the emphasis of Six Sigma on reducing variation. Interestingly, processes need to be flexible, and not rigid, to get rid of volatility in customer experience. Peaks and troughs are inherent in many real-life businesses and processes. For example, salespeople across the globe seem to be consistent in bringing in the bulk of their business toward the end of the day, month, quarter, and year (and taking it relatively easy the rest of the time). The challenge for the business is how to balance their process capability so that they end up being neither under-equipped during the peaks nor wastefully over-equipped during the troughs. This is one of the areas where Lean concepts such as multiskilling, *heijunka*, and effective inventory management can combine with Six Sigma to provide a winning solution.

> *Processes need to be flexible, and not rigid, to get rid of volatility in customer experience.*

## THREE TYPES OF LEAN SIX SIGMA PROJECTS

Having been involved in over a thousand Lean Six Sigma (LSS) projects over more than a decade, I find that improvement projects can be broadly categorized into three types: quality improvement, revenue enhancing, and cost saving.

> *Improvement projects can be broadly categorized into three types: quality improvement, revenue enhancing, and cost saving.*

## Quality Improvement Projects

The quality improvement project is the quintessential LSS project. This project typically attacks a defect or customer complaint and seeks to eliminate or reduce or, ideally, prevent the defect. Relevant data are usually available for such projects. The *heart* of this project is analysis of the data to find out the root cause of the defects. Once found, the root cause is eliminated by a change or improvement in the process so that the problem doesn't recur. This process change is typically some form of poka-yoke or mistake-proofing.

## Revenue-Enhancing Projects

We were pleasantly surprised to find that LSS projects were extremely effective not only for reducing defects or improving quality for customers, but also for directly increasing revenue. Examples of such projects are activating inactive distributors, getting repeat business from existing customers, or increasing first time right (FTR) sales. Our experience with revenue-enhancing projects was that they usually need only the most basic Lean or Six Sigma tools. However, they often involve a change in behavior and mind-sets. For companies that are up to this challenge, these projects can yield enormous business results. We found that such projects typically involve putting some basic discipline or process in place where none existed before, and putting some simple in-process measures in place where previously only the end output (sales or revenue numbers) was being measured.

For example, one company that sells through distributors realized that a large number of distributors were inactive, that is, they hadn't sold anything for the last several months. While the company knew they had a problem, they were unable to get a handle on it. They tried to solve the problem through traditional methods (such as senior sales managers yelling at junior salespeople, and junior salespeople yelling at distributors) but without any results.

When all else failed, the CEO decided that he had nothing to lose if he threw the problem as a challenge to the Lean Six Sigma team. When the same problem was taken up as an LSS project, the focus shifted from people (as in whom to blame) to the issue. The moment it became an LSS project, three things were done differently than before. First, they put in place a standard definition of what exactly the company meant by "inactive distributor." It may sound basic, but the fact was that several companies had no standard definition, and "inactive" meant different things to different people within the same company. Second, a simple process was put in place. The process would kick in the day a distributor became "inactive" according to the company's standard definition. The process itself was nothing revolutionary—it typically would involve two or three simple steps, such as a salesperson from the company contacting the distributor with a standard script, inquiring if there was any problem that the company could help the distributor with (salespeople were trained to use this script—contrast this with the earlier practice of yelling matches), and a joint visit to a prospective client by the distributor and the company's salesperson. Third, in-process measurement began. Where earlier only the end output of sales or revenue numbers was measured, now the company started measuring the number of distributors who fell into the inactive funnel each week, and how many of the inactive distributors went through the "reactivation" process that was now in place. It was mandatory to measure and report this each week.

Our experience in every single business that did such projects has been that the bit of discipline that the process brings, and the focus on the right enablers, results in significant and sustained improvement in revenue. In fact, the revenue results from several such projects were so significant that we couldn't believe it ourselves at first. Some of us wondered whether this would have happened *anyway*. We did a little experiment. In one company, 29% of the previously inactive distributors became active after they went through the LSS process. We compared this with another "control group" of inactive distributors. The distributors in the control group had not yet been through the LSS process. There was no other difference between the two groups. At the end of the same period, the percentage of distributors from the group that did not go through the LSS process that became active was 0.8%. Compare that with 29% for the LSS group and imagine what this can do for your revenue!

Another kind of revenue-enhancing project is to increase FTR sales, which we saw in the last chapter.

## Cost-Saving Projects

These projects typically are concerned with eliminating waste. We found that after training employees on simple Lean concepts, such as the nine types of waste and value stream mapping, they are able to look at their own work process to identify possible wastes and eliminate them. We also found useful the practice of systematically looking at top expense items on the company's financial statements to see if one or more of the types of waste had crept in and could be removed. Here again, an organizational culture of accountability and waste-consciousness, with senior management walking the talk and setting personal examples, can go a long way.

It is important to remember that waste elimination and "cost cutting" are as different as chalk and cheese. A big difference is that waste elimination is a proactive measure, while cost cutting is usually a reaction—often part of desperate measures for desperate times. In companies like Toyota, we learned that waste identification and elimination is a continuous, never-ending activity. On the contrary, cost cutting is often a one-time activity. Another big difference is that the benefits of waste elimination sustain in difficult times as well as in good times. Perhaps the biggest difference is that waste elimination is *not* at the cost of customers or employees. How can anything that hurts customers or employees be good for your business in the long run?

> Waste elimination is not at the cost of customers or employees. How can anything that hurts customers or employees be good for your business in the long run?

## HOW TO SELECT AND PRIORITIZE LSS PROJECTS

We followed a simple practice of sitting down with the CEO and their senior executives at the start of each year, and again in the middle of the year, to understand their business priorities and business problems that needed to be attacked on priority. Customer complaints, the annual customer satisfaction survey, and the internal quality dashboards formed additional sources from which LSS projects would be identified. The company's financial statements showing various types of operating expenses were a useful source to identify cost-saving projects. At times, employees would just come up with an idea for a new LSS project in their business or functional area. We would create a list of "candidate" LSS projects based on all these inputs, which we would discuss again with the CEO to select the final list of top-priority projects. While selecting the final list of projects, we would try and ensure that each company had a mix of all three types of LSS projects described earlier.

Some companies use more formal methods such as *quality function deployment*, or *house of quality*. This is a structured method of listening to and understanding customers' needs and using this knowledge to design products, services, or solutions (asq.org). The same approach can be used to identify and prioritize LSS projects based on business priorities. You may use a formal method if you find it useful. In essence, it is also a way of identifying and prioritizing projects that will contribute to achieving the business's priorities.

## DO NOT MARRY A MODEL

Don't get me wrong, I don't mean to poke my nose into anybody's matrimonial plans. I am talking about those companies that seem to get obsessed with a particular model or methodology to the extent that the model overshadows real and sustained business results. It is also important not to jump from fad to fad. Our experience is that any of the known models, if adhered to consistently and in the right spirit, without losing sight of business results, is bound to deliver results. What matters is that you believe in the model you are following—be it Lean or Six Sigma or ISO 9001 or total quality management or plan–do–check–act (PDCA) or a combination that suits your organization—and, more importantly, stick with it.

A business leader once ridiculed ISO 9001, saying, "Even the municipal office of this city is ISO certified. And we all know how inefficient they are! I don't believe ISO can do my business any good." Now, I happen to know several companies that have achieved significant business results and process excellence through ISO 9001. In the municipality example, it is not ISO's fault, but the spirit in which ISO 9001 was implemented that is to blame. They just wanted the ISO 9001 certificate; nobody in the organization was genuinely interested in customers or process excellence. Then why blame the model?

It is important to remember that the model is not your end objective, but your means to achieving business results. Despite knowing this, if some of us wish to be seen as implementing a business excellence model without the intent to actually achieve excellence, we are only fooling ourselves!

> *It is important to remember that the model is not your end objective, but your means to achieving business results. Despite knowing this, if some of us wish to be seen as implementing a business excellence model without the intent to actually achieve excellence, we are only fooling ourselves!*

## WHAT TO DO WHEN CUSTOMERS COMPLAIN

What do you do when your customers complain? Some people try to hide (the complaints) from their boss! The next few chapters share lessons we learned about what to do and what *not* to do when customers complain.

# 11
# Is a Complaining Customer Doing You a Favor?

*A complaint is a gift.*

—Janelle Barlow

## THE CUSTOMER'S STORY

I'm a customer. One morning, I visited my bank for a small transaction that should have taken about two minutes. However, there was a big queue and I was number 27 in line! So here I was, all set to spend the next hour or more waiting in line for something that should have taken a couple of minutes. But worse was to come. About a half hour later, the employee at the counter decided to take a break. She told the waiting customers that she would be back in 20 minutes. Some customers protested, but she told them curtly that they could come back the next day if they weren't prepared to wait! Saying this, she disappeared into an inner room. In fact, this was my fourth visit to this bank for the same transaction. My work remained unfinished as the bank had some problem or the other every time.

I thought to myself, "Should I send a formal complaint?" I was of two minds. It didn't seem worth the trouble writing a complaint. Then I asked myself, "Why am I even dealing with this bank? Especially when other banks are falling over each other to get my business?" In fact, I already had an account with another bank that provided much better service. I didn't even need this bank account!

In about three minutes, my decision was made. It was easier for me to just stop giving business to this bank and close my account. Why bother with writing a complaint? Looking at their attitude, it seemed unlikely that they would do anything about it, anyway. To me (the customer), the employee at the counter *is* the bank. Her attitude is the *bank's* attitude.

In a few days, I closed my account with that bank. And I am not missing them at all.

## THE BANK'S SIDE OF THE STORY

Of late, we've had trouble keeping our customers. The worst part is that most of them don't even bother to tell us what the problem is—they just go away! We wonder why.

We do get a few customers who send us formal complaints, but we are sure those are isolated problems. After all, among thousands of customers, there will always be a few who are never satisfied. Troublesome pests! We can't spend our time looking at these isolated cases.

However, we've just gotten approval for a substantial sum of money for a big television ad campaign. We are sure that once we spend so much on advertising, customers will come back and business will pick up.

## THE BANK'S STORY SIX MONTHS LATER

We just went bankrupt! We're closing down because we don't have any customers left! How we wish we had listened to those customers who took the trouble to complain and tell us what the problems were. But we thought they were pests! We now realize—too late, alas—that while most of our customers experienced poor-quality service, only a tiny minority bothered to tell us about it. The vast majority just left—without a warning! We realize now what a big favor those complaining customers were trying to do us—if only we had taken them seriously!

## THE CUSTOMER (AS ALWAYS) HAS THE LAST WORD

That's it. For me, and for many other customers as well, it's easier to just take our business elsewhere—even easier than writing a formal complaint. Businesses need to realize that handling a complaint from a customer is more the company's requirement than the customer's requirement—assuming the company wants to survive. So do *yourself* a favor and remember that the customer who complains is not being a pest, but doing you a big kindness.

> **Handling a complaint from a customer is more the company's requirement than the customer's requirement—assuming the company wants to survive. So do yourself a favor and remember that the customer who complains is not being a pest, but doing you a big kindness.**

# 12

# Resolved, but Not Resolved

*A complaint isn't resolved until the customer says so.*

A company with a large customer base has a monthly practice of measuring its performance on quality- and customer-related metrics. These are reviewed each month by the CEO and the rest of the senior management team. These measures are part of the performance appraisal of senior management.

Among the important measures that form part of this monthly review are measures related to customer complaints. One of these measures is the percentage of complaints that were resolved within the target time the company had set for itself. Month after month, the performance graphs showed over 99% on-time resolution. The source for these data was the company's customer relationship management (CRM) system, in which all queries, requests, and complaints from customers are entered and tracked until resolution. Consistently, month after month, over 99% of the complaints were reported as resolved on time.

## A RIDDLE

Surprisingly, the CEO, as well as the group chairman, got fairly frequent e-mails from customers about their complaints. The company's customer service head brushed these off, saying that some customers just wanted to create a sensation by writing directly to the CEO or chairman instead of going through "proper channels." However, the CEO noticed that in almost every one of these e-mails, the customer mentioned that they had initially tried one of the "proper channels"—either the company's customer service phone number or e-mail. Some had even visited the company's offices. They had escalated their complaint to the CEO or chairman only when they did not get a resolution to their complaint after waiting for a considerable number of days or weeks.

This set the CEO thinking. "Why would so many customers write to me or the chairman saying that their complaints are not resolved, when over 99% are resolved on time?" he wondered aloud.

Dev, a member of the senior management team, asked, "But how do we know that 99% of complaints *are* resolved on time?"

CEO: "What do you mean? Aren't you present at the monthly performance reviews where these data are shown?"

Dev: "Yes, but what is the source of these data?"

CEO: "Why, our CRM system, of course! You know we spent a fortune on the new CRM system just a few months ago. Now, Dev, I hope you're not suggesting that our new CRM system isn't any good, are you?"

Dev: "Boss, the data are only as accurate as the person who enters them wants them to be, aren't they?"

CEO: "Now what are you trying to get at, Dev? Do you mean to say that our people are entering false data into the system?"

Dev: "I wouldn't want to make a guess on a serious issue like this. But why don't we find out?"

"How?" The CEO was getting impatient with Dev throwing questions at him instead of trying to help with answers.

Dev: "That should be easy enough. Why don't we just ask the customers who complained."

The CEO glared at him. He was getting a little irritated with Dev talking in riddles. Dev explained, "We can do a little audit. Let's take a sample of complaints that have recently been tagged as 'resolved' in our CRM system and ask the customers who made those complaints if their problem was actually resolved."

Over the years, the CEO had never ceased to be surprised at Dev's unusual methods. But he had developed a healthy respect for the ability Dev had demonstrated on several occasions in the past to cut through the internal cobwebs and see things from the customer's perspective.

## AT LAST, SOME LIGHT

Two weeks later, the sample audit was complete. The CEO called a meeting of the customer service head and other members of the senior management team.

"Do you have any answers for us, Dev?" started the CEO. "Why are so many customers writing to me and to the chairman saying that their complaints are not resolved?"

Dev: "Well, yes—it's simply because they are, er, *not* resolved!"

Seeing the blank faces in the room, Dev continued, "Somebody is just tagging them as 'resolved' in the CRM system. That means nothing to the customer unless the complaint is actually resolved, does it?"

The customer service head sounded hurt, "Are you trying to accuse me and my team of dishonesty?"

Dev felt tempted to make a rejoinder, but he decided to avoid any personal remarks and just stick to the audit findings and evidence. He continued to the group, "Let me explain how we did this audit. First of all, don't forget that we selected random samples *only* from cases that were already tagged as 'resolved' in the CRM system. Next, we looked for case details, resolution comments, and evidence of resolution in the CRM system itself for each of the samples. In almost every case, if one went just by the resolution description and evidence available in the CRM, there was no evidence of the complaint having been resolved from the customer's point of view . . ."

The customer service head couldn't wait to defend her team, "Well, given the large number of queries, requests, and complaints that we get, I admit there may not be time to write full details of resolution of each case in the CRM system. But that doesn't mean that complaints are not resolved!"

"That brings us to the next step in the audit," Dev continued, "We assumed exactly what you just said, and actually spoke to the customers to find out if they had gotten a resolution to their complaints. In more than 50% of the cases, the customer said that neither had their complaint been resolved, nor had they even heard anything from the company about their complaint. And, mind you, we are talking about cases that were tagged as 'resolved' days or weeks ago!"

Dev then went on to give examples from several common types of complaints. These included cases where money or some document was to be received by the customer (such as an insurance claim, a refund, or a document, or a commission payment due to an agent, and so forth). In all the cases, the customer's side of the story was similar—"I am still awaiting resolution of my complaint. In fact, I haven't heard anything from them. I wonder what's taking them so long"—or words to that effect. And, according to the company, each of these cases was resolved and closed.

There was silence in the room when Dev paused. The CEO was the first to find his voice, "But how can this be? How could the CRM system show all these complaints as 'resolved' when they've not been resolved for the customer who complained?"

"I am able to explain that now because I found the answer while doing this audit," said Dev. "During the audit, we also spoke to the employees from our company who tag the complaints as 'resolved.' We realized that every person and every department is in a tearing hurry to 'meet their TAT (turnaround time)' so that their performance graphs look good. Everyone is looking at their bit of the problem, and once they have hit the ball into someone else's court, it's not their problem anymore."

"Let me give an example," continued Dev. "In the case of a claim to be paid to a customer, the claims department found that the claim was genuine, but a document was required from the customer before the claim could be paid. Getting the document from the customer was the responsibility of Sales and not Claims. But leaving the complaint's status as 'open' in the CRM system would show the claims department in a poor light. So they just went ahead and tagged the complaint as 'resolved' with a comment saying 'awaiting document from customer.' There are other types of complaints, too, but the underlying attitude seems to be similar. Each of us inside the company is in a big hurry to show 'resolved within time' on our individual or departmental performance graph. In over half of all complaints, a status showing 'resolved' in the CRM system doesn't mean that the customer has gotten the resolution—it only means that one person or department within our company has moved the monkey from their back to another person or department within the company, or back to the customer!"

## OTHER "SMART" WAYS OF BEATING THE SYSTEM

Dev also unveiled some other innovative ways people were using to beat the system and make their performance graphs look good. Some twisted the definition of "resolved" to mean what was convenient to them or their department, as described above. In some other cases, a complaint was tagged as resolved before the target date, and another complaint for the same problem was entered in the CRM system on a later date. This way, at no point in time would the complaint appear to have exceeded the target time. A third "smart" practice was to categorize complaints as "queries."

## THE FINAL OUTCOME

"But whom are we trying to fool? Customers have choices, and they are just going to leave us if this is the way we treat them!" thundered the CEO. "The complaints data is for *us*—it tells us the health of our business. Falsifying complaints data is like falsifying your medical reports to make yourself feel good—it could eventually kill you!"

Sadly, the CEO was right. The symptoms had been ignored for so long, and the disease had grown so big, that the company never recovered from it. A few years ago, this company was in a rapid growth phase, pumping in money to open new offices, recruiting more salespeople every day, and adding nearly 30,000 new customers each month. Today, new customer additions have trickled down to a few hundred a month. Existing customers are leaving. And guess where the customers are going? To competitors, who *don't* tag customer complaints as "resolved" until they are actually resolved—according to the customer.

## THE LESSON

Only short-sighted companies would want to make some inward-looking dashboard look good and, in doing so, lose their customers, as well as miss the opportunity for real, continuous, permanent improvement. I call this disease (yes, that's what it is—a disease) "resolved but not resolved" (RBNR). Some companies allow the problem to grow so big that it eventually kills them!

The lesson from this company is the importance of being prompt about resolving issues from the customer's perspective. Smart companies will even go a step further to find out the root cause of the problem and use it as an opportunity for continuous permanent improvement. The next chapter is about how to get to the root cause.

# 13

# Root Cause Analysis

*Ask why, not who.*

Dev had recently joined a large company in a senior management position. On his first day on the new job, the HR manager welcomed Dev and showed him his new office. It was a nicely fitted, well-equipped cabin with large glass windows. Dev liked his new office and felt that it would provide him the perfect environment to do his job well.

The next morning when Dev entered his new office, a somewhat foul smell hit him. He now vaguely remembered that he had noticed the same smell the previous day, too, but hadn't paid much attention to it. The HR manager had occupied his attention the entire first morning, explaining company policies and introducing him to people. After she left him, Dev had been busy meeting his team members. Perhaps with all this, his nose got used to the strange smell by noon and failed to notice it any more. But today, the smell was unmistakable.

Dev looked around the office, including under his desk, to see if he could find the source of the smell, but could find nothing. At the precise moment when Dev was examining the space under his desk, his bubbly colleague Ava walked in with her loud greeting, "Good morning Dev . . . what're you doing down there?" Slightly embarrassed, Dev quickly sat up, banging the back of his head on the underside of the desk in his haste. Ava left Dev's office a couple of minutes later, but not before she remarked, "Dev, do you notice a strange smell in your office? Maybe you should get the admin people to do something."

After some hesitation (it was only his second day and he didn't want to be seen as a "complainer"), Dev spoke to the admin manager Raj. "It's impossible, Sir. We have an office cleaning contract, and the entire office is cleaned daily and kept spic and span. Anyway, I'll come and take a look." That afternoon, Raj visited Dev's cabin, and took a few deep breaths.

Raj (reluctantly) admitted that *indeed* there was an "unusual" smell. "Don't worry, I'll fix these rascals." Before Dev could blink, Raj had summoned one of the cleaning contract staff to Dev's office. Raj shouted, "Can't you smell this foul odor? What kind of cleaning do you guys do? I want you to fix this immediately."

Almost trembling with fear, the poor cleaning guy ran out. He returned a minute later with two more cleaning staff. Each of them was armed with a can of air freshener. They sprayed all over the office until their cans were nearly empty. It sure smelled good now! When they had left, Raj turned to Dev, "There you are. The problem is fixed now." He went on to explain that it wasn't the fault of the admin department. "It's an external contractor, you see. We have to kick them to work. But they have a tough customer in me." He was evidently proud of the way he had made the contractor's staff do the job. Dev thanked Raj—the office did smell good now.

That afternoon, Dev took his team out to lunch. He thought this would be a good way of getting to know his new colleagues better. Ava recommended this new restaurant she had checked out with her friends the previous week. They had a great lunch. Back in office after a leisurely lunch, as Dev entered his cabin, he was surprised— the same old foul smell had returned. A weak trace of the lavender spray lingered, but the old stench was clearly overpowering it.

"We will terminate the cleaning contract with your company," Raj roared on the phone at the cleaning contract company's manager. Ava, who had peeped in on hearing the din, suddenly looked up with her nose pointed toward the ceiling and remarked, "The smell seems to be coming from above. Could it be coming through the air conditioning vent?" Raj was somewhat irritated. "I've been in this office for two years and nobody has told me about bad smells from the air conditioning!" But Dev said, "She might be right, Raj, there's no harm checking. In any case, we've looked everywhere else and that seems to be the only place left. It's hard to work with this foul stench, and I would really appreciate your help." "If you insist, Sir, I will get the air conditioning vent checked," said Raj.

The next morning, a small team from an air conditioning maintenance and servicing company came. They got about their business of checking the air conditioning vent and ducts. Dev sat in the next room to try and get some work done with his team in the meanwhile. About an hour later, they heard a shout from Dev's cabin. "We got him!" In a moment, one of them came up to Dev and said, "We found what was causing the smell. You had a visitor!" They had found a dead lizard inside the duct, which was causing the smell. The lizard was removed. They had found a small hole in the duct, through which the lizard had obviously entered. They worked until afternoon to seal the hole.

After the maintenance team had left, Raj paid Dev a visit. "You're all set, Dev! Sorry about the trouble, but you will agree, one can hardly blame Admin for this. Whoever would have expected a lizard to enter the air conditioning duct!" Raj almost seemed to think it was the lizard's fault.

Dev was relieved that he could finally work in his office without inhaling lizard-scented air, but the whole episode had gotten him thinking. "Thanks, Raj, why don't you join me for a cup of tea?" Over tea, Dev remarked, "Raj, I believe we have offices on several floors of this building." "That's right, we have offices on seven floors," replied Raj. "I think you're doing a great job—I can appreciate it's not easy to manage admin for such a large company." Raj was evidently pleased with the compliment. Dev continued, "I was thinking about the hole in the air conditioning duct. Since we have offices and central air conditioning on almost every floor in this building, do you think there could be similar holes elsewhere?"

Raj: "I don't think we need to worry. After all, nobody else has complained."

Dev: "I am still just curious to know how come there was a hole in the duct and it was not detected."

Dev's previous company had regular preventive maintenance for their plants and equipment, including air conditioning systems, and Dev assumed this happened everywhere.

Next day, Raj spoke to the building owner and discovered that no maintenance work on the air conditioning had been done in the last eight years, except fixing anything that broke down.

Dev suggested, "Why don't we get the same maintenance company that found the lizard to inspect and overhaul the air conditioning system in the entire office. They seemed to know their job." A few weeks later, with Dev's gentle persuasion, the company got this done for all their offices in the building. Several more holes and other defects in the air conditioning system were detected and repaired. The maintenance experts told Raj and Dev that they had been wise in deciding to get the inspection done now—better late than never. The preventive repairs would help the company avoid more disruptive and expensive breakdowns that would certainly have happened otherwise.

Dev had a final question, "Are you now sure that a similar problem will not arise in future?"

To this the experts replied, "We are confident that there will be no problems immediately, but in the long run, you need to have a regular preventive maintenance inspection done once every six months. This will help prevent expensive breakdowns. A preventive maintenance contract costs only a fraction of what most common breakdown repairs can cost."

A few weeks later, the company put in place a process for preventive inspection and maintenance of its air conditioning systems. The process was documented and signed off. Raj the admin manager was appointed as the "owner" of the preventive maintenance process.

Dev decided to play the cynic. "Are we actually going to do this every six months, or is the process going to be just on paper?" he asked Raj with a wicked smile. Ava had a suggestion, "Why don't we have an independent process compliance audit for the preventive maintenance process? We can have somebody from outside the admin department audit the process every six months to check for evidence that the preventive maintenance, as described in the process document, has actually been done."

That was five years ago. The company has adhered to the preventive maintenance process and has never again had any trouble with the air conditioning. A calculation by the accounting department showed that the company had actually spent more on air conditioning breakdown repairs in two years before preventive maintenance started than had been spent on preventive maintenance in these five years.

They all lived happily ever after (except the lizard)!

# THE TECHNIQUE OF ROOT CAUSE ANALYSIS

If you have understood the lizard story (by the way, it's a true story), you have understood the technique of *root cause analysis* (RCA) and are ready to apply it to defects or complaints in your own organization (or at home, for that matter). The root cause is identified using the familiar *why–why* or *five whys* or *five whys and one how* method

| What happened | What was done (Corrective action) | Will this *prevent* this problem from happening in future for *all* customers? |
|---|---|---|
| Customer (employee) complained | | |
| Foul smell in office | Housekeeping staff sprayed air freshener | No |
| | Housekeeping staff blamed, warned, and fired | No |
| Dead lizard in AC vent | Dead lizard removed | No |
| Gap/hole in AC vent | Gap sealed | No |
| No maintenance done for last eight years | Overhauling of all AC ducts done | No |
| No process for periodic preventive maintenance exists | Process for proactive checking and preventive maintenance every six months put in place and *implemented* | Yes |

**Process compliance audit:** The preventive maintenance process will be audited every six months to check for *evidence* of adherence to the process

**Figure 19** Example of root cause analysis through the why–why or five whys technique.

(see Figure 19). The question *why* is asked five times (actually, there is nothing sacrosanct about five, the idea is to continue asking *why* until you reach the root cause). Once you have reached the root cause of the problem, ask *how* to eliminate the root cause to prevent the problem from happening in future. The complete cycle of how RCA works is shown in Figure 20.

This method was made famous by Toyota, where the five whys analysis is an integral part of *kaizen*, or continuous improvement (Liker 2004). Toyota's approach has been adapted in the lizard example above. While the lizard story is intended to explain RCA in an easy-to-understand way, this chapter is based on the experience of applying the same technique to a number of business problems (including customer complaints). Some examples of business results

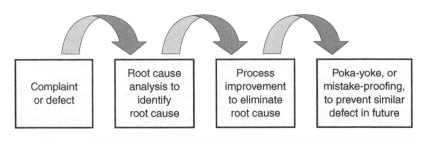

**Figure 20** The cycle of root cause analysis.

from root cause analysis in companies that I have been associated with follow.

## SAMPLE BUSINESS RESULTS FROM ROOT CAUSE ANALYSIS

The technique of RCA described earlier is disarmingly simple. In fact, when we train people on RCA, a typical response at the end of the training is "that's *it*?" Despite its simplicity, we have found RCA to be one of the most potent tools in terms of business results (no wonder RCA is a fundamental element of the Lean philosophy, which is about "getting more with less"). Companies that I have worked with have successfully applied RCA to dozens of business problems. Two of these real examples of business results from RCA are described below.

*Example 1.* An investor in a mutual fund informed the company that they had received a duplicate redemption payment (*redemption* is when an investor sells their investment in the mutual fund for cash). The company did RCA, identified the root cause of the problem, and built a preventive control into the redemption process. In a one-year period after the RCA and process improvement were done, the company made over a million redemption payments, with a total value of about 70 billion dollars. And—because of the RCA and elimination of the root cause of the duplicate payment problem—the company knows for sure that there is not a single case of duplicate payment. For the period before the RCA, the company has no data and is not sure about how many duplicate payments went out. At these business volumes, even if duplicate payments happened in a fraction of a percent of the total number of transactions, the financial loss to the company would be enormous. Thus, the business benefit from RCA is obvious.

*Example 2.* A securities brokerage provides online securities trading accounts to its clients. The client's trading account is linked to their bank account. If there is a change in the bank account (such as a change in the bank account number, or if the client wants to link a different bank account), the client sends a request to the company, which is normally processed within four days. Ninety-nine percent of these client requests were followed by a complaint because the company was unable to process the requests within the promised time. Following the RCA and implementation of process improvements identified through the RCA, the complaints came down from 99% to 6%!

In both these examples of business application of RCA, the approach used to get to the root cause was exactly the same as in the lizard example. That's how simple it is—and look at the business results!

## CRITICAL SUCCESS FACTORS— LESSONS LEARNED IN ROOT CAUSE ANALYSIS

Years of experience applying RCA to dozens of business problems taught us many lessons. We also made quite a few mistakes. Hopefully, we have learned from these, too. Listed below are what we found to be critical success factors for RCA to be effective. I have also talked about our mistakes, so that you don't make them (or, at least, have a good laugh at our expense).

1. *Stopping before getting to the root cause.* We saw how, in the lizard story, we almost stopped at several stages *before* getting to the root cause—once after spraying the air freshener, then after the lizard was found and removed, and again after fixing the hole in the air conditioning duct. At none of these stages had we actually reached the root cause, which was the absence of preventive maintenance. We were merely attacking the symptoms instead of getting to the root cause and eliminating it. This happened in several business problems as well; we sometimes found ourselves almost unwilling to get to the bottom of it. In some cases, we were fortunate to have someone like Dev who gently pushed us along. In others, we learned the hard way—the defect kept recurring, or customers continued to complain, forcing us to eventually identify the root cause and eliminate it.

2. *"We did the RCA but there is nothing to change in the process."* Time and again, we found that despite doing the RCA and identifying opportunities for improving the process, there was resistance to actually making the process change (or introducing a new process where none existed, as in the lizard example). We were happy to take one-time actions like removing the lizard or even fixing the hole in the duct, but committing to the discipline of following a process repeatedly in future seemed daunting. Or was it the accountability the process would bring that we were secretly afraid of? Unfortunately, as we learned, the improvement could never be permanent unless the *prevention* of the root cause is institutionalized. And any institutionalization means going back to the process. In other words, we learned that RCA without process improvement is meaningless.

> **RCA without process improvement is meaningless.**

We realized from experience that there seemed to be only two types of *how* (to eliminate the root cause) for any problem—process or people (often both). By *process*, we mean an absent or faulty process. By *people*, we mean that the process exists on paper, but it was not followed. This, in turn, could be due to lack of either training or discipline. In manufacturing industries, the cause could also be defective machines or parts or raw materials, but these can also usually be traced back to either a process issue or a people issue. Once the correct root cause is identified, the solution is either to introduce a process (if no process exists), or improve the process (if it is faulty), or train/discipline people to follow the process. Wherever possible, *poka-yoke*, or mistake-proofing, possibly using technology, can be used to minimize the chance of human error. A familiar example of mistake-proofing in computer data entry is the use of an online calendar to select a date instead of actually typing in a date—which significantly reduces the chances of entering a wrong date.

> **There seemed to be only two types of how *(to eliminate the root cause)* for any problem—process or people (often both).**

3. *Identify the root cause, not "whom to blame."* One of the biggest hurdles on the road to the root cause is the tendency to mistake the question *why* for *who*—as in "who did it?" We often found people trying to fix the blame for the problem rather than get to the root cause. We had to repeatedly tell (and prove to) people that the company was not interested in knowing whose fault it was, but only in preventing the problem from happening again. This has a lot to do with organizational culture. It is senior management's responsibility to make everybody comfortable discussing defects and complaints without getting into a blame game.

> *One of the biggest hurdles on the road to the root cause is the tendency to mistake the question* why *for* who—*as in "who did it?"*

Companies like Toyota actually encourage employees to make quality problems visible. They even empower workers to stop production, if necessary, as soon as they detect a defect, to fix the problem (immediate correction), as well as for root cause analysis for preventive steps (Liker 2004).

4. *"That's outside our control."* This is another common roadblock to root cause analysis. The moment the *why–why* trail led us outside our own department or our company, we tended to drop it, saying (often with a sense of relief), "That's beyond our control, there's nothing we can do." Almost every business problem we encountered involved more than one department within our company, and often, external entities such as vendors, distributors, and partners to whom certain types of work were outsourced.

After months of losing improvement opportunities on the pretext of "third-party dependency," one day somebody gathered the courage to ask "So what?" Why couldn't we get the relevant "outsiders" (other departments or external third parties) to work with us to identify the root cause and reduce defects? We laughed at the person who suggested this, but let her go ahead and try it anyway (we couldn't wait to see her get egg on her face).

The first time this was tried was with an external company to which some key processes were outsourced. In the past, most customer complaints used to be blamed (conveniently) on this "third party." To everybody's surprise, at our request this external partner was happy to work with us in reducing defects and customer complaints. We knew they were serious when they deputed to be part of the root-cause analysis team three of their best people, who were experienced with the process they were running for us. Both companies found that not only did working together help reduce and prevent several types of customer complaints, but also brought productivity improvements and cost savings. Such benefits are shared by both companies, increasing profits for both.

5. *"But nobody's complained before."* The best time to do RCA and eliminate a defect is as soon as it is first detected. However, defects often don't get the attention they deserve until customers start complaining. In some cases, we almost refused to accept the existence of a defect—until customers forced us to. Like Raj in the lizard story, even *after* complaints started to surface, we would sometimes respond, "but nobody's complained before!" I have seen some cases where, despite getting several complaints, each time our response would be that "nobody's complained before!" We sometimes needed a flood of complaints to start actually paying heed to a defect. In the process, we lost time, money, and, at times, customers.

6. *"But that's the standard practice."* A common response we get once the root cause and solution are identified is "but that's the way it's always been done," or "that's the industry practice." The preventive action to eliminate the root cause of most problems is a process change or behavior change, and—as with any other change—there is often resistance. We learned from experience that the best way to manage this change is to make sure that the people who actually "do" the process are involved in the RCA. This way, they are part of the solution rather than the problem.

7. *Losing the way (or losing the* why*)? Have the right attitude. Use the template. Ask the customer. Observe the process.* In some cases where RCA was being done, we would discover that we had lost our way or reached a dead end at one of the *why*s. There would be no apparent further answer to "why?" nor would the point we had reached look like a root cause with a clear preventive action. For example, an insurance company was getting a number of customer complaints about errors on policy documents. The company decided to find out the root cause to help them reduce the errors. The RCA team's answer to the first *why* to this problem was that there were errors in some of the application forms submitted by the customers in

the first place. These errors were carried over to the policy document. The answer to the next *why* (why were there errors on the application forms?) was that customers completed the forms in a hurry (who likes to fill out forms?). Most of the team members felt there was nothing we could do about customer behavior. Some of them said that this RCA was getting us nowhere. Errors on some insurance policy documents was a "normal industry practice" that we just need to live with, they added.

Fortunately, one team member said, "Wait a minute! Is there *really* nothing we can do? Is the customer being in a hurry really the reason for the errors? After all, the customer is more interested than anybody else in getting an error-free insurance document, so why would so many of them be hasty and put wrong information on the application form? Why don't we speak to a few customers who complained and find out what really happened?"

When we did this, we realized that we had gotten the answer to the first *why* wrong! The customers we spoke to told us that they had never filled out the application form in the first place. The company's agents who sold them the insurance had asked them to just sign the blank application and collected certain mandatory documents for proof of age and address. The agents had told the customers that they would fill in the details later at the company's office to save the customer the trouble. As the agent was usually known to the customer, most customers would agree to this.

The RCA team then decided to directly observe what the agents did next. Some of them visited the company's office and observed agents who were there. Several agents were hurriedly filling out the application forms on behalf of the customer. They would rely on their own knowledge or the documents provided by the customer (some of these were barely decipherable photocopies). The agent's priority, of course, was to hand over the application to the company and collect their commission. The RCA team realized their folly—they had lost their way by answering the first *why* wrong. The correct reason for the errors was not that the customer was completing the forms in a hurry, but that the customer was not completing the forms at all—it was the agent, based on second-hand knowledge, who did this on their behalf.

Once the real cause was identified, the RCA team realized that there *was* something the company could do about it. The preventive action in this case was to make it mandatory for agents to get the form completed by the customer and educating all agents about this.

The company saw a drastic reduction in the errors and complaints when this was done.

We learned from this example that it is important for the RCA team to have the right *attitude* of prevention, not blame. To arrive at the right answers to each *why*, the people doing the RCA must never forget that they are trying to identify what can be done to prevent the problem. Blaming someone outside our circle of influence may be convenient, but will usually lead to a dead end, as in this example. An easy way to avoid this is to pause for a moment after answering each *why* and ask, "Does this really explain *why* the previous step happened, *and* is it leading us closer to finding out how to prevent this problem?" Do this *before* asking the next *why*. Using a simple template for RCA (see Figure 19) helps a great deal to stay on the right path.

> *It is important for the RCA team to have the right* attitude *of prevention, not blame.*

We also learned from this experience that two easy ways of arriving at the root cause, or at least remaining on the right path to the root cause, are to *ask the complainant* for more details and to *observe the process* as it actually happens. Some of us were at first afraid of speaking to customers who had complained, but we found after talking to several customers that most of them actually appreciated the fact that the company was taking their complaint seriously and involving them in the prevention efforts. Several customers said that the company's efforts to eliminate defects at the root gave them more confidence in the company despite their recent bad experience, and promised more business in future.

   8. *Drill-downs or Pareto charts are not root cause analysis.* In the insurance policy error example discussed earlier, somebody did a "drill-down" (in this case by geographic location) and identified the error percentage in each city where the company sold insurance. This was shown as a Pareto chart, which helped identify which locations contributed the majority of errors. While such a drill-down is very useful, it is important to remember the difference. While Pareto charting or drill-down can help us identify *where* to focus from among a large number of possible categories (for example, the top few cities that account for the majority of errors in this example), the RCA will help to identify *why* the defects happened so that they

can be prevented. Used in tandem, Pareto charts and RCA can be a potent combination.

9. *Identify the problem right.* This is the most obvious first step to a meaningful RCA. Wrong problem identification is not uncommon. It can lead to waste of time and resources in "preventing" a problem that does not exist! We learned from experience that wrongly focusing on an individual rather than the issue (for example, in the lizard story, if the problem had been wrongly identified as "troublesome new employee" instead of "foul smelling office") or jumping to a conclusion (for example, in the insurance example, if the problem was identified as "hasty customers" instead of "errors on policy documents") are the two most common causes of wrong problem identification. It is important to identify the problem right *before* asking the first *why.*

10. *Root cause is different from "source."* It is important to distinguish between the immediate source of the problem and the deeper root cause. The lizard was the "source" of the bad smell, but, as we saw, the root cause was the absence of a preventive maintenance process. The problem will go away permanently only if the root cause is eliminated.

11. *There could be more than one root cause, or "RCA branches."* We found that in a few cases, there were two answers to a *why.* In such cases, the RCA may branch off into two streams as we further try to find the root cause for each of these answers. For example, a wrong diagnosis in a hospital had two parallel causes: faulty equipment *and* a poorly trained technician. The root cause of the first was a faulty preventive maintenance and calibration process for equipment, while the other was due to a flawed staff training process.

12. *Keep it simple.* We learned the importance of keeping the RCA simple and practical. When we introduced the RCA template (see Figure 19), some of us got carried away and would fill in all kinds of (mostly irrelevant) details in the template. Remember, the end objective is to identify the root cause and take real action on the ground to prevent the defect from recurring. Filling in the template is just a means to guide our thinking logically to get to the real root cause. Experience taught us the importance of keeping the RCA template brief, to the point, and action oriented.

13. *Spend time to think—do not jump to conclusions or action before you have finished thinking.* At Toyota, it is said that problem solving is 20% tools and 80% thinking (Liker 2004). In our

businesses, we at times found ourselves impatient to act before completing the RCA. Halfway through, we would think we knew the answers and get into action. In every one of these cases, we found that we had actually lost time (and, at times, money) by not spending enough time to think. When our actions did not make the defect or complaints go away, we would be forced to go back and identify the *real* root cause. Our experience after numerous RCAs is that the *how* (identifying the preventive action) is usually the easy part. Once we get to the correct root cause, the preventive action usually suggests itself.

14. *Have an open mind.* Experience taught us the importance of being open to all possibilities and not having any foregone conclusion in our minds before or while doing the RCA. After all, if the answer were so obvious, the problem might not have happened in the first place. In some cases, we thought we already knew the root cause and merely used the RCA template to justify our views (this is like a root cause looking for a problem rather than the other way around). Needless to say, this did not make the problem go away, and we would eventually have to go back and do a real RCA.

15. *Involve relevant people.* Some of the most effective RCAs we ever did—that identified practical solutions and gave lasting business results—were the ones where people actually involved in the relevant process on the ground were part of the RCA team. We would have a facilitator (usually a person from the quality department) to moderate the discussion toward the root cause. The facilitator could also ask thought-provoking or out-of-the-box questions that might not occur to people involved in the process day in and day out. At the end, however, the answers would usually come from the people involved in the process. This way, also, their buy-in or willingness to actually implement the process changes identified through the RCA would be high. It was *their* idea, after all!

16. *Have a genuine intent to get to the root cause.* This sounds obvious, but you would be surprised by the number of times we saw teams go through the "ritual" of RCA without ever intending to get to the root cause. Some of our businesses made RCA mandatory for customer complaints. The company's aim was to use complaints as opportunities for continuous permanent improvement. However, for several complaints, we found that the RCA template was religiously completed (on paper), while more of the same type of complaint continued to occur. We learned an important lesson here—it

is important to genuinely *intend* to get to the root cause and eliminate it!

> ***It is important to genuinely* intend *to get to the root cause and eliminate it!***

17. *Addressing peripheral issues rather than the main root cause.* In some cases, even after the main root cause had become obvious, we found people reluctant to do anything about it. Instead, they would make a pretense of taking some action by addressing some secondary issue. Obviously, the problem would never go away unless the main issue was addressed.

For example, an insurance company received numerous complaints from customers about delays in receiving their policy document. RCA revealed that most of the delays were due to errors on the customer's application form or a missing mandatory document (such as a proof of age) required with the application. These required subsequent rework (to correct the error or to get the missing document), which led to the delay. Thus, the root cause was applications not being right the first time. It was the responsibility of the sales teams and agents to get first time right applications. However, in this company, Sales was a "sacred cow" that couldn't be burdened with mundane stuff like first time right. So they found some peripheral issues like trying to make the operations teams process the applications faster or correct the errors faster (instead of *preventing* the errors in the first place). Naturally, the problem didn't go away. The defects and complaints were increasing month after month. After losing several months this way, the company was finally left with no choice but to address the root cause. Salespeople and agents were trained on how to submit first time right applications, and part of their bonuses was linked to this. When the root cause was thus attacked, the company saw a dramatic reduction in the defects.

18. *Hiding defects from the customer.* In a majority of customer complaints, the company was actually aware of the defect even *before* the customer complained. We were just hoping that customers would not notice.

For example, a company found that its sales agents were paid their commission at a lower rate than was due to them. This was due to an error in the commission processing system. The company kept silent, hoping that the agents wouldn't notice the error. It was only when they were flooded with complaints that they woke up. Many agents felt cheated and left the company to work with competitors. Another company with a similar problem informed their agents about the error the moment it was detected, and apologized. They promised to compensate them in the next month (which they did). The agents really appreciated this. Several of them said that by informing them about the error proactively, the company had won their trust, and that they would never work for a competitor, even if they were offered a higher commission. The second company had actually turned a problem into an opportunity!

After several such experiences, we realized that in every defect, there were actually two defects. In the example above, the first defect is the wrong commission, while the second defect is not informing the agents *before* they complained. We started doing RCA for *both* defects. Over a period of time, this helped the businesses put in place a process of proactively informing customers about defects *before* they became complaints. While we would find it daunting to inform customers about our defects, we would be pleasantly surprised every time at how the customer actually seemed to appreciate this gesture rather than get upset about the defect.

19. *Measure the outcome.* It is important to measure the impact of the RCA and preventive actions. The best way to measure the impact is to compare the defects or complaints before and after. This measurement is the only evidence that shows whether an RCA has had the desired outcome. We also found that thus measuring the impact after each RCA helped convince everybody in the company about the benefit of RCA to the business, and institutionalize the culture of getting to the root every time we have a problem.

## TESTS TO FIND OUT IF YOU HAVE REACHED THE ROOT CAUSE AND ELIMINATED IT

How do you know whether you have actually reached the root cause? This is sometimes not as easy as it seems, as our various mistakes show. At the same time, this is extremely important, as we may expend considerable cost and time to eliminate the root cause, and you don't want to do this for the wrong root cause. Secondly, it is not enough to just find out what the root cause is—you also need to eliminate it.

Once you think you have reached the root cause and eliminated it, applying the following simple tests will tell you whether you are actually there:

1. Ask yourself if you have actually reached the root cause. Are there no further answers to *why*? Our experience in most cases was that when you reach the root cause, the solution (the *how*) almost automatically suggests itself.

2. Ask if you have identified what needs to be done to eliminate the root cause and prevent the problem from happening in future.

3. The biggest test, of course, is to see if the problem or defect or complaint has gone away. I have lost count of the number of times we thought we had done a great RCA and eliminated the problem, but customers wouldn't stop complaining. Every time this happened, we were forced to go back and ask the two questions above. In every single case, we found that the answer to one, or both, was *"no."*

## RCA—THE EPITOME OF LEAN

The beauty of root cause analysis lies in its simplicity. As a former Toyota executive said with some sarcasm, "We have a very sophisticated technique. It is called five why. We ask why five times" (Likert 2004).

One could say that RCA is the epitome of Lean. What other technique is so simple to understand, yet so big on results? No continuous improvement is possible without RCA. Doubtless, there are certain requirements to obtain real, substantial, and sustained results from RCA. These have been dealt with in detail in this chapter, and clearly, they mostly have to do with discipline and the right mind-set. For organizations (or individuals) that have this discipline and mind-set, defects and complaints become opportunities that propel them forward on the journey toward excellence!

*No continuous improvement is possible without RCA.*

## CAN PROBLEMS BE PREVENTED *BEFORE* THEY EVER OCCUR?

So far in this chapter, we have talked about how to use a defect or problem, after it occurs at least once, to get to the root cause and prevent the problem from happening again. In a few of the companies that I worked with, somebody would ask, "But do we always have to wait for a problem to happen, and then prevent it? Can't we anticipate what *could* go wrong and prevent it even *before* it happens?" A very useful question, and our experience on this is as follows.

These companies used a simple practice of calling people involved in the process into a meeting and trying to identify everything that *could* go wrong. In other words, what were the risks or "failure modes" in the current process—for the customer or for regulatory compliance? In addition to identifying potential failure modes, answers to the following questions would also be discussed: Is there a way to do this process at a lower cost? Is there a way we could do this more efficiently? Often, some opportunities for improving the process would be identified this way. We used a simple two-way matrix (see Figure 21) to prioritize what improvements

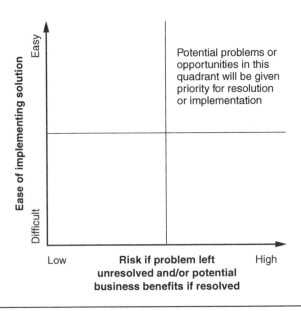

**Figure 21** Matrix for identifying and prioritizing problems *before* they occur.

or process changes should be done immediately. Top priority was given to changes that would bring higher benefits, or carried higher risks if not done, and were relatively easier to implement.

We found this proactive approach to be extremely useful, and several process improvements were made even before a problem could hit us. Obviously, we were unable to anticipate *all* problems or defects. For problems that did occur, we did the next best thing—get to the root cause and prevent the problem from happening in future.

Smart companies have a combination of both—the proactive approach to anticipate and prevent problems before they *ever* occur, and RCA and future prevention for problems that do occur. Not-so-smart companies will let the same problem happen again and again, usually until their customers decide to do something about it—like walking out!

> **Smart companies have a combination of both—the proactive approach to anticipate and prevent problems before they ever occur, and RCA and future prevention for problems that do occur. Not-so-smart companies will let the same problem happen again and again, usually until their customers decide to do something about it—like walking out!**

# 14
# Close the Loop with the Customer

*Are you living in a different world than your customer?*

A sales agent phoned the call center of a large company that she sold for. She had not received her commission for the last month. "We're sorry about this ma'am, we will surely look into it and get back to you," said the call center executive. The executive created a "service request" in the company's CRM system and entered the agent's complaint.

Three weeks later, this complaint happened to get picked as part of a random sample audit of the complaint-resolution process. The status of the complaint was tagged as "resolved and closed" in the CRM system. The resolution comment against this complaint in the CRM said, "Commission dispatched, hence, the complaint is closed." The comment had been entered by Linus from Finance who was responsible for commission payments.

Dev, the auditor, phoned the agent just to confirm whether she had received her commission. "No, I'm still waiting." The agent's voice seemed to hide just a trace of irritation.

Rather perplexed, Dev went back to Finance. "Hey, Linus, why did you say 'resolved' in the CRM when the agent says she hasn't got the money?" Linus gave Dev a funny look, "My friend, our job in Finance is to dispatch the commission. Don't tell me you expect me to call every agent and ask them if they got their money. I've done my job. Don't you know our commission process runs at Six Sigma efficiency?"

The company's practice was to calculate commission centrally at headquarters and dispatch the money to each branch office (the company has over a thousand branches). An operations person at each branch would hand over the commission to agents attached to their branch.

Dev was determined to get to the bottom of the mystery. He phoned the branch manager. The branch manager said, "I doubt if we've received the agent's money. Are you sure Finance sent it? They never send the commission on time, and then blame us when agents complain about getting their money late."

When Linus heard the branch manager's accusation, he was livid. "If you don't believe me, I'll show you the proof of dispatch." The next morning, Linus showed Dev an airway bill from the courier company, which was proof that the courier had picked it up from Finance. Linus had spent half a day to dig up the proof.

Dev persisted, "But the agent is complaining that she didn't *get* the money. She isn't complaining that you haven't *dispatched* it. I agree that you have proof that it has been dispatched, but what if it somehow hasn't reached her?" It was like talking to a wall. Linus showed Dev the commission process document, "Here, look at the process document. It says that the last step is to dispatch the commission—and I have done that. I have followed the process to a T. I can't be held responsible for things that are outside my process!"

Dev's head was reeling. He decided to wait for a couple of days. Perhaps the agent might receive it by then. Two days later, he called the agent again. The agent again denied having received the commission. "Are you sure ma'am? I have seen the proof of dispatch myself," Dev asked. Now the agent sounded somewhat annoyed, "Why don't you ask your own colleague who claims they gave me the commission? I wish you people would just pay me my money that was due weeks ago, instead of calling me again and again. It seems to me that people in your company don't talk to each other."

Dev went back to Linus. Now that Linus had proof that he had dispatched the commission, he had covered himself and refused to spend any more time talking about the agent's problem. However, he was determined to get even with the branch manager. He passed the buck right back. "Dev, didn't I show you the proof of delivery? If you've got nothing better to do, why don't you ask the branch what they did with the commission? I'm sure they're sitting on it."

Dev called the branch manager again. "Dev, this is a complete waste of our time. You have no idea how busy we are at the branch.

Anyway, since you insist, I'll have somebody check and get back to you."

When no one called for two days, Dev called the branch again. This time, the branch manager's tone was a tad softer. "Sorry, we did receive the commission. It's in my safe. Not to worry, we'll give it to her next time she comes to the branch."

When Linus found this out, he confronted Dev, "See? I told you we had dispatched it. Obviously, the complaint is resolved. As far as Finance is concerned, we are running at Six Sigma efficiency and we can not let the branch people's inefficiency spoil our measurement." The minor detail that the agent didn't have the money in her hands seemed irrelevant to Linus. What mattered to him was to make his charts look good. But Dev decided to deal with Linus later. He had another question for the branch manager, "But why haven't you given the money to the agent? She's been complaining and seems quite upset."

"She *complained*? Why didn't anybody tell me that?" asked the branch manager. "Anyway, what's there to complain about? My operations person just forgot to give it to her. Her money is safe with us!"

Dev called the agent. "Ma'am your complaint is resolved. We found your money. Your commission was processed long ago. It's lying safe with the branch. They just forgot to give it to you." Dev thought she would be relieved. However, this time her irritation seemed mixed with amusement. "Son, do you think it makes a grain of difference to me whether the commission is processed or not, or if it's lying at your headquarters or at the branch? And, what do you mean my complaint is 'resolved'? All that matters to me is that I haven't received my money till now, and I should have had it weeks ago. To me, my complaint will be resolved only when I get my money in my hand."

When Dev got back his composure (and this took some time), he realized that this agent had just taught the company a most important lesson. Clearly, the customer (the agent in this case) couldn't care less about the process followed by the company or what anybody in the company said about where the money was lying. The only thing that mattered to her was whether she had the money in her hand. To make matters worse, somebody in the company had tagged her complaint as "resolved" while she had yet to even hear from the company about her complaint. How could anybody call her complaint resolved unless she, the complainant, told them that it was resolved? She felt cheated.

Dev reflected some more and realized that it was not anybody's "fault." Some juicy blame games and passing of the buck did happen between Linus and the branch manager, but the person who had complained didn't show the least interest in knowing whose fault it was. She was only interested in her complaint being resolved.

Then it struck Dev that what was really missing here was "close-looping with the customer" (*customer* here means the person who complained). The company had tagged the complaint as "resolved" without actually resolving it from the customer's perspective, and without even bothering to check with the person who had complained. Was this because the person (or department) who tagged the complaint as resolved was not responsible for the end delivery to the agent? The job of Finance, after all, was merely to send the commission to the branch office. It was the branch that was responsible to actually hand it over to the agent.

Should the company then put the responsibility to tag such complaints as resolved on the branch managers instead of Finance? "I am willing to take the responsibility, provided my TAT (turnaround time) starts when the branch receives the commission. Obviously, cases where Finance delays sending the commission can't show as open complaints against me. After all, that's not my fault," said the branch manager. So here was a new challenge. While Finance was unwilling to own the problem once the commission had left their hands, the branch was willing to own it only after it had reached the branch. Nobody in the company was looking at it end to end. But, unfortunately, end to end was the only way that the customer looked at it. To her, nothing else mattered.

Having spoken to the customer and heard her point of view, the absurdity of it all struck Dev. Here was everybody in the company working hard to make their measures look good (and, in the process, even tagging unresolved complaints as resolved), while none of this added any value to actually resolving the problem from the customer's point of view, which, in this case, was simply for the agent to get her money.

Dev continued to think. Could it be possible that many more "commission not received" complaints from other agents were similarly tagged as "resolved" in the company's CRM system without actually resolving them? And could other types of complaints from end customers or agents also be meeting with the same fate? Dev sank into a sofa under the weight of his thoughts.

During the next few days, Dev did a quick sample audit of other common types of complaints received by the company. The audit itself was simple enough—all Dev needed to do was to pick a random sample from each type of complaint that was tagged as "resolved" and ask the complainant to confirm whether their complaint was actually resolved.

The audit confirmed Dev's fears. In a large proportion of every type of complaint, the customer who had complained denied having received any resolution. They said that they were still waiting for the resolution, and many of them were plainly angry that it was taking the company so long to resolve their complaint or even respond to them. And, mind you, we are only talking of complaints tagged as "resolved."

Dev found another fishy practice. It was bad enough that a large number of complaints were tagged as "resolved" without actually resolving them. There was another bunch of complaints that were tagged as "rejected." On probing these, Dev found that these were cases where, in the opinion of somebody in the company, what the customer was asking for was not doable. For example, an insurance claim that is genuinely not payable going by the terms of the insurance policy would be promptly tagged as "rejected." Dev spoke to a few customers whose requests or complaints had been "rejected" over a month ago. Each of them said that they had not heard anything from the company and were awaiting a resolution or at least a response from the company. Dev told these customers that what they were asking for was not doable and explained the reasons. He did this with some trepidation, expecting the customers to get mad at him. But he was pleasantly surprised to find that most customers were quite understanding when the facts were honestly explained to them. Several of them actually said they appreciated that the company was at least taking the trouble to talk to them and "close the loop"—even if their request could not be met.

## THE MEETING WITH THE CEO

Dev sought a meeting with Amla, the CEO. "You'll have to make it quick, Dev. I have an important meeting with our sales heads. We're losing customers and market share, you see, and I need to plan our strategy to counter this."

Dev began, "That's interesting, Amla, and I may have part of the answer to why we're losing market share." And Dev went on to fill the CEO in on what his audits and conversations with customers had revealed. He also told Amla about the "resolved" and "rejected" complaints in the CRM system.

Dev concluded, "So, I'm afraid the charts you have been shown month after month showing certain processes running at near Six Sigma efficiency and on the number of customer complaints and the percentage of complaints resolved on time—all these have very little to do with reality. Most of these charts are merely someone in the company telling us that they (or their department) have done their part. All the individual charts look good—but nobody is telling you what the customers are saying."

Amla had been listening intently all along with a statuesque expression. He seemed to be lost in thought for several moments even after Dev had stopped speaking. When he spoke, it was evident that what he had heard had shaken him. "This is an eye-opener, Dev! No wonder our customers are leaving us in droves. I'm still going to have that meeting on why we're losing market share. But in addition to the sales heads, I want you to be there. Also, call everyone else from the management team who has a role to play in resolving issues commonly raised by customers or agents."

The meeting on market share turned out to be a session led by Amla in which he laid down what he called the "commandments" for dealing with any problem brought by customers or agents. The commandments were based on the lessons learned from the story so far about the agent's complaint.

The commandments would be relevant in almost any business in any industry, and are given below.

# THE COMMANDMENTS (LESSONS LEARNED)

1. *The customer must say it's resolved. Never* tag a customer's complaint or query as "resolved" or "closed" until the person who complained says so. In other words, "close the loop with the customer." Every company must figure out the most practical way to do this; for example, for routine queries and requests, a random sample of customers may be contacted (independent of the person or department who said "resolved" in the CRM system) to get a confirmation that their query was resolved. For complaints, every complaint must be close-looped with the customer before tagging it as resolved.

> **Never *tag a customer's complaint or query as "resolved" or "closed" until the person who complained says so.***

2. *Don't say "resolved" to make your charts look good.* Before tagging a complaint as "resolved," ask yourself "resolved for whom—your department or the customer?" Are you saying "resolved" based on some action that puts the ball in someone else's court, but doesn't yet resolve the issue for the customer? Are you saying "resolved" to make some inward-looking measurement charts look good?

3. *Take end-to-end responsibility.* Do not pass the buck. For each type of query, request, or complaint, one person must be responsible for the end delivery to the customer. This person must be accountable to the customer. This person will have end-to-end responsibility. Often, they will need to cut across departmental boundaries, but remember, the customer does not care (and why should they?) about your internal departmental structures. The person responsible for end delivery to the customer must have internal service-level agreements with others within or outside the company on whom they depend for ultimate delivery to the customer.

4. *Give the same person the right and the responsibility.* The person who has the right to tag a complaint as "resolved" must be responsible for hearing from the customer that it has been resolved. This can bring huge competitive advantage. The very fact that some competitors think this can not be done is an opportunity for others who do—and will.

5. *Do not generalize.* Instead, look at each specific case (remember how the branch manager in this story says that Finance *never* sends the payments on time, without even bothering to look at the individual case).

6. *Talk to the customer even if you can not fulfill their request.* Even where we can not do what the customer is asking for, explain the reasons to the customer and close the loop. Most customers will appreciate the company having gotten back to them, even if their request can not be fulfilled.

7. *Talk to each other—don't make the customer repeat the story.* People (often from different departments) from the company must continuously talk to each other while resolving a customer's problem. Do not make the customer repeat their story every time they speak to somebody from the company.

8. *Fix the issue, not the blame.* Always remember, the customer does not care about whose fault it is, but is only interested in getting their problem resolved. Fix the issue without getting into a blame game.

> **The customer does not care about whose fault it is, but is only interested in getting their problem resolved.**

9. *Let the customer decide the medium of communication.* The customer will decide how they want to communicate with the company—e-mail or phone or visiting the office. Do not tell the customer to use any other way of communicating (often, a customer who phones is asked to send an e-mail or visit the office, a customer who walks into an office may be asked to contact the company's call center, and so forth). Leave the choice of medium of communication to the customer. As far as possible, close-loop using the same medium—for example, a customer sending an e-mail would expect an e-mail response. For more serious issues or complaints, an additional phone call to the customer to confirm resolution would always be appreciated by the customer.

10. *Take the ownership of the issue* and continue to be responsible and proactive. Do not try to dodge the issue by putting the ball back in the customer's court. If you need something from the customer to be able to resolve the issue, go to the customer and get it, but don't stop until the customer tells you the issue is resolved.

11. *Make sure your processes are defined end to end from the customer's perspective.* The easiest (but useless) way to run a process at Six Sigma efficiency is to cut out the customer

and eliminate everything that is "outside my control." (In the story here, the last step in the commission process must be not someone *dispatching* the commission, but the agent *receiving* the commission. If this were done, Linus's process efficiency would no longer be at Six Sigma).

## WHAT'S *YOUR* COMPANY'S CULTURE?

In your company, do customer issues or complaints get tagged as "resolved" without actually resolving them from the customer's perspective? This can be dangerously misleading, because you will not get to know the real picture as to how many customer issues or complaints were genuinely resolved on time, how many were resolved late, how many still remain unresolved, and how old the unresolved ones are. If you don't get to know this, obviously this can't be a focus area for your company. Because these "early warning signals" remain hidden from you, you may get the picture only when the problem manifests itself in the form of more serious outcomes such as customers and business leaving you. By then, it may be too late—or definitely much more difficult—to reverse the situation.

In the company in this story, once the Commandments were in place and enforced, gradually, the company's culture started changing. People slowly started taking ownership of customer issues until they were actually resolved from the customer's perspective. The behavioral and culture change was a slow process. But, little by little, customers and market share started coming back. Everyone in the company realized the importance of closing the loop with customers to retaining their customers and market share.

# 15
# Kaizen and the Power of Ideas

*Are you wasting your people's ideas?*

In the last several chapters, we discussed the role of performance measurement, listening to customers, and quality improvement projects using the Lean or Six Sigma methodology. While there is no denying the importance of these as sources of continuous improvement, we realized that this is only half the story.

What about people and their ideas? We found that not all improvements necessarily happen through formal projects. Our people (including employees, partners, and even distributors) and their ideas proved to be an equally powerful source of *kaizen*, or continuous improvement. For example, in a five-year period in a large group of companies, the direct financial results (revenue and cost savings) derived by collecting and implementing ideas from their people was as big as the total results from large, formal Lean Six Sigma projects.

> *We found that not all improvements necessarily happen through formal projects. Our people (including employees, partners, and even distributors) and their ideas proved to be an equally powerful source of kaizen, or continuous improvement.*

In this group, nearly 25,000 ideas were generated during this period. After a process of evaluation and selection, about 15 percent of the ideas ended up getting implemented. Many ideas were from employees suggesting small (and occasionally large) improvements in their own work process or in customer service. Several were cost-saving ideas. Some were revenue ideas as they related to new products or market expansion. About 30 percent of the implemented ideas had a direct financial benefit in the form of either revenue or cost savings. In this five-year period, ideas contributed 550 million dollars in revenue and another 120 million dollars in cost savings to the group! In the same period, larger and more formal Lean Six Sigma projects contributed 580 million dollars in revenue and 70 million dollars in cost savings.

The contribution of continuous permanent improvement initiatives was too significant as a percentage of the group's total revenue and profits for anybody to ignore. And, mind you, the financial numbers above are the result of a mere 30 percent of the total ideas implemented and the approximately 40 percent of the total number of Lean Six Sigma projects that had a *direct* impact on revenue or cost on the company's financial statements. A larger percentage of ideas and projects were related to process improvements or customer service. Clearly, these would also result in financial benefits in the medium term (through customers staying with us because of good service or long-term cost benefits through more-efficient processes), though they are not reported in the numbers above.

And did you notice that the contribution of ideas to financial results is as big as larger Lean Six Sigma projects? So, how could we afford to ignore our people and their ideas?

The absolute number of ideas and financial results will obviously differ from company to company depending on geography, industry, size, and other factors, but there is no denying the power and potential of ideas. If you are curious to know how these businesses generated so many ideas and how they are sustaining the inflow of ideas (don't ideas dry up after a time?), our experience is shared below.

## A SHAKY START

Let me begin with a confession. When we started off, some of us were skeptical ("we've seen suggestion schemes before—they never work . . ."). The rest of us were a little more indulgent ("no harm trying it out . . ."). Obviously, very few people expected any serious business results from this, and not in our wildest dreams did we expect the kind of results that we're now talking about. In fact, the whole "ideas thing" would have died a natural death in its infancy if it were not for one business leader who genuinely believed in the power of people's ideas. "We have 18,000 employees and thousands of partners and distributors. Is it so difficult for each person to come up with one idea once in a year—at least a small idea related to their own work or business? Especially if we share the rewards with them?" he asked. Nobody could argue with that! So, perhaps that's the first lesson—for significant and sustained business results from ideas, the first requirement is at least one senior genuine believer or "champion."

Next, very few people believed that this new "scheme" would last more than a few months—a year at best. Even after seeing results beginning to come in, many people thought it was only a question of time before the ideas dried up. Here, again, our experience has been the opposite. Far from "drying up," in the fifth year the number of ideas generated as well as implemented was higher than in any previous year. Here's the story of how this happened.

## A PROCESS FOR IDEAS AND INNOVATION—AT TWO LEVELS

I don't believe there is anything radically new in our approach. Nevertheless, since it gave the businesses significant results, I thought it might interest you.

Like many other companies, we launched a simple employee suggestion scheme. We called it *IdeaExpress*. An initial launch communication from the CEO was sent to all employees, followed by fairly regular repeat communications. A "suggestion box" in the form of a common e-mail ID or portal where people could send their ideas was created. Each business created an "evaluation committee"—typically a group of senior executives from a variety of functional backgrounds—to evaluate and select ideas for implementation.

One of the things that we did to keep ideas relevant and increase the probability of ideas getting implemented was to announce certain "themes" from time to time. The themes were based on current business priorities, and people were encouraged to come up with ideas related to these themes.

We introduced reward and recognitions at employee, team, and company levels to reward them for giving and implementing innovative ideas that would benefit the business. Some businesses offered a share of the actual revenue or cost savings achieved through the idea. These rewards were given in a visible manner to the winning employees in the presence of their colleagues. We have been giving these rewards every half year for nearly five years. I believe this has helped us to convince employees that the company is genuinely interested in their ideas.

In our experience, one of the biggest factors responsible for the results from this initiative, and their continuity, is the fact that it is mandatory for every business in the group to measure and report the number of ideas collected, selected, and implemented, and their business results (see Figures 22 and 23 for sample summary and detailed report formats). As we have seen in an earlier chapter, what gets measured gets managed better and gives better results.

| IdeaExpress Report | April to June 20xx |
| --- | --- |
| Number of ideas gathered | |
| Number of ideas selected for implementation | |
| Number of ideas implemented | |
| Number of ideas where implementation is in progress | |
| Cost savings from implemented ideas | |
| Revenue from implemented ideas | |

**Figure 22** Sample summary report of ideas generated and implemented.

| Idea number | Idea description | Employee name | Business benefits |
| --- | --- | --- | --- |
| 1 | | | |
| 2 | | | |
| 3 | | | |
| 4 | | | |
| 5 | | | |
| 6 | | | |
| 7 | | | |
| 8 | | | |
| 9 | | | |
| 10 | | | |

**Figure 23** Sample detailed list of implemented ideas.

We got a large number of small ideas and a small number of large ideas through the IdeaExpress suggestion scheme. The numbers proved that the sum total of results from the small ideas was so huge that it would have been foolish to ignore them or to focus exclusively on large or "breakthrough" ideas.

> *The sum total of results from the small ideas was so huge that it would have been foolish to ignore them or to focus exclusively on large or "breakthrough" ideas.*

## INNOVATION PROCESS FOR LARGE BUSINESS IDEAS

That said, one of our businesses simultaneously introduced, at another level, a process for large business ideas. At the start of one year, the CEO created a cross-functional "Innovation Council" consisting of eight senior executives. They roped in an external consultant—an "innovation expert" who specialized in coaching on "innovative thinking." The consultant conducted a coaching session for 40 selected people, along with the CEO and the Innovation Council members. This is my personal opinion, but I suspect that more than teaching any specific "techniques" the most useful aspect of this coaching was merely to make us *unlearn* our traditional way of thinking—often limited and clouded by years of specialization in a narrow functional area—and to make our minds less cynical and more open and willing to look at new ideas and possibilities.

For the first year, the CEO decided that he would like to first use this process of innovation for new product and business ideas so that they could quickly test, through tangible results, whether the innovation process worked. "After all, what measure is more tangible and easily understood than revenue?" he reasoned.

Following the coaching session, the group of 40 was broken up into eight teams of five people each. Each team was given a month to come up with at least a couple of new product or business ideas, with a complete business plan on how and in which markets they planned to sell, the projected revenue, costs, and profits. The teams spent much of this month on the road, visiting existing and potential markets, talking to customers and distributors, and observing what competitors were doing. After several brainstorming sessions among themselves, they generated 20 business ideas. Like an entrepreneur presenting a business idea to a venture capitalist, the teams presented their ideas to the CEO and the Innovation Council. Eleven of the 20 ideas were selected for implementation. The teams that came up with the ideas were also made responsible for implementation. The company would invest in or "incubate" these business ideas. The teams were promised a share in the profits. A year later, eight of the 11 implemented new business ideas were successful and had made a reasonable profit, with significant growth expected in the coming year.

While this company happened to use the innovation process for business or revenue ideas in the first year, in subsequent years they successfully used the process for breakthrough innovations in new processes, customer service, operations, and other areas.

The IdeaExpress and the Innovation Council approaches resulted in a variety of business benefits, ranging from new products and capturing new markets or customer segments to improvements in service, processes, productivity, and cost savings. Some of our most successful new products were the result of our people's ideas, gathered through our innovation process. During the financial crisis of 2008, IdeaExpress was one of the biggest contributors to saving costs and protecting the businesses' profitability—because our people came up with a large number of cost-saving and waste-eliminating ideas. In fact, there is hardly any functional area or other aspect of the businesses that did not benefit from capturing and implementing people's ideas. We would have lost most of these ideas if we didn't have IdeaExpress as a platform for people to share their ideas.

## CONTINUOUS PROCESS FOR INNOVATION

Our experience in this group of companies busted a myth or two about innovation. Some of us thought innovation was the job of only a few people (you may know some companies that have an "innovation department" with pony-tailed innovators who dream up new ideas). While not undermining the importance of this, we learned that ideas that were good for the business could come from anyone. What is needed is a process that encourages everybody who could be a potential source of ideas to *continuously* share their ideas, a process that ensures that you do not lose any idea that could be good for your business, a process to evaluate, select, and implement them, and a way of measuring the results. As we saw, the company in this example has one process at a mass level for the IdeaExpress suggestion scheme, and a slightly different process for bigger ideas. You may use a similar approach, or have your own process. Our experience clearly showed us that innovation is a *process* more than anything else. And, in any case, the innovation process has no conflict with somebody occasionally dreaming up a completely "out of this world" breakthrough idea, even outside the process—the process will not prevent them from doing so.

> *Our experience clearly showed us that innovation is a process more than anything else. And, in any case, the innovation process has no conflict with somebody occasionally dreaming up a completely "out of this world" breakthrough idea, even outside the process—the process will not prevent them from doing so.*

## WILL IDEAS DRY UP?

Another myth that got busted is that ideas would dry up after a time. Some of us expected employees to run out of ideas after the first six months or a year at the most. As one CEO put it after the first year of IdeaExpress, "Whatever ideas could come, have come—so let's shut down the scheme."

To my mind, this is like saying, "Whatever business was to be done has been done—so let's shut down the company!"

In reality, however, the number of ideas actually increased year after year. In our fifth year, we got more ideas than in any previous year. I realized that we weren't the only company to experience this. I had an opportunity to visit a cigarette manufacturing company that won an award for its employee suggestion scheme. They told me that the scheme was in its seventeenth year! Again, what seems to separate these companies from others where ideas dry up after a time is that they have a *process* to sustain and motivate continuous idea generation and implementation—in areas that are relevant to the business and customers. And they continuously communicate with their people to inform them about current business priorities and specifically solicit ideas in areas that are important to the business at that time.

## YOUR COMPANY'S CULTURE CAN EITHER ENCOURAGE OR KILL INNOVATION

Initially, we found that the committee in charge of evaluating employees' ideas rejected almost every idea saying, "So, what's new?" or "What's so innovative about this?" or "But they're supposed to be doing this *anyway!*" Many of us probably feel this way about every idea except our own! The committee members had to be coached that we were not necessarily looking for "first time in the world" innovations every time. The right questions to ask are "Will this benefit the business and customers?" and "Is it already being done in our company?" Logically, every idea where the answers to these two questions are yes and no, respectively, must be implemented—of course after evaluating feasibility and cost.

> *The right questions to ask are "Will this benefit the business and customers?" and "Is it already being done in our company?" Logically, every idea where the answers to these two questions are yes and no, respectively, must be implemented—of course after evaluating feasibility and cost.*

We also went through another learning experience. Many of our senior colleagues had worked for years in organizations where there was no culture of encouraging employees to come up with ideas. In those cultures, employees were there just to obey orders. Thinking and developing new ideas was the job of "management." Ironically, some of the best and most practical ideas (naturally) came from people on the ground and not from the ivory tower people. A few months after we launched the suggestion scheme, some employees came to us and complained, "That was my idea. It has been implemented, but the company never acknowledged that it was my idea."

We realized what was happening. Quite a few ideas were being taken out of the suggestion box, selected, and implemented—but some senior staff were reluctant to give credit to the person whose idea it was (especially if that person was a junior from their own team). We got over this culture problem by making it mandatory for every CEO and senior functional leader to implement a certain minimum number of ideas from their people.

We learned that an important responsibility of senior management is to create a culture where people feel motivated to continuously think and come up with new ideas. The only way to do this is to communicate and prove to your employees that you are genuinely interested in their ideas. We found it useful to have a mandatory process of acknowledging every idea received. We realized that even in cases where it was not feasible to implement an idea, it was important to explain the reasons to the employee who gave us the idea. This way, the employee remains motivated to come back with new ideas, even though their last idea could not be implemented.

## THE IMPACT ON PEOPLE AND MORALE

Apart from the business benefits from implementing people's ideas, we experienced a very positive impact on employee morale. I have personally had employees come up and tell me after we introduced the IdeaExpress scheme, "I have been here for years, but it is only now that the company has started listening to me and my ideas. I was always paid a salary for my work, but now I feel that the company values me."

## WHAT MADE IDEAEXPRESS DIFFERENT FROM THE STANDARD "SUGGESTION BOX"

I am sometimes asked if there is a "secret sauce" behind IdeaExpress. Do we have a unique system or process? What makes it different from the standard "suggestion box"?

As for the nuts-and-bolts of how the scheme works, the process we use to generate and evaluate ideas, and so forth—I don't believe it is any different from suggestion schemes in many companies. I have briefly described our process in this chapter.

I suspect that what makes IdeaExpress different (helping these companies achieve significant business results, and continuing to do so year after year) are:

1. *Business leader's belief.* To my mind, one of the strongest reasons for the sustained success of IdeaExpress is a business leader who genuinely believes in the power of people's ideas, and what these ideas can do for the business.

2. *Strategic importance.* IdeaExpress is a strategic initiative that is regularly discussed at the leadership and even at the board level. This shows the importance attached by senior management to this initiative. In addition, CEOs and other senior executives demonstrate to employees, through their communications and actions, that they are serious about IdeaExpress and have high expectations of people's ideas.

3. *Making senior staff accountable.* Senior staff such as departmental heads are made responsible to encourage their team members to come up with new ideas, and to ensure that every employee in their team contributes at least one small or big idea once a year. It turns out that these ideas are usually related to the employee's own work or process, and at times, related to other areas that are relevant to the business. The message to senior staff is clear, "You are expected to behave *not* like policemen and shut out your people's ideas, but like gardeners who nurture and encourage the free flow of ideas."

4. *Regularly measuring and publishing results.* I believe this is one of the biggest reasons for the sustained success of IdeaExpress. Details such as the number of ideas generated and implemented, quantified business results, the names of the employee or team who contributed and implemented the idea, and so on, are compiled and published without fail every month. Every company in the group has published their results from IdeaExpress every month for about six years now, without missing a single month. Seeing the results published gives everybody in the company, including the senior management, confidence and further strengthens their belief in the initiative, leading to continued participation and results. In a sense, this is a self-sustaining cycle—seeing the results motivates higher levels of participation, which, in turn, leads to further results, and so on. We actually

experienced this. The monthly report is also a great way to give credit to employees who give and implement ideas. Publishing the monthly IdeaExpress report (see Figures 22 and 23) is mandatory in these companies, just like publishing their financial statements.

5. *Rewards, recognition, and acknowledgment.* These companies regularly (twice a year) reward and recognize employees who contribute and implement ideas that give good results. The best idea-generators are rewarded in a visible way, in the presence of other employees. Even if an idea is found not feasible to implement, it is acknowledged, and the employee who contributed the idea is encouraged to keep coming back with new ideas.

6. *Keeping it always relevant to the business.* Having "themes" from time to time, where ideas related to a particular business priority or issue are particularly solicited, helps the companies to keep IdeaExpress always relevant to their current business priorities.

7. *Not a "soft" initiative.* In quite a few companies, a suggestion scheme tends to be a "soft" initiative, perhaps aimed at making employees believe that their voice is being heard. No one really expects any serious business benefits from the scheme. In such companies, the "suggestion box" often tends to be a "black box" into which ideas disappear, never to be heard of again. Why should anybody then be surprised when such a scheme fails or dies a premature death? IdeaExpress is radically different from such farcical schemes in that it is a "hard" strategic business initiative. Participation of employees is, of course, the backbone of the scheme, but it is seeing their own and their coworkers' ideas actually being taken seriously, implemented with business results, and acknowledged, that encourages employees to keep coming back with more ideas.

## CONCLUSION

The whole point of this chapter is to share an important lesson we learned—that employee ideas can be a rich source of continuous permanent improvement, and can give business results that are as big as what you can get through more formal improvement methods like Lean and Six Sigma. Our experience is that it is best to pursue both in parallel; have a process for continuous innovation and idea generation on the one hand, and use a structured methodology like Lean Six Sigma on the other. I must mention here that some of the bigger or more complex ideas were implemented in the form of formal projects. In other words, some of our Lean Six Sigma projects originated as somebody's idea.

> *It is best to pursue both in parallel;*
> *have a process for continuous innovation*
> *and idea generation on the one hand,*
> *and use a structured methodology like*
> *Lean Six Sigma on the other.*

# 16

# 360-Degree Knowledge Management

*Imagine the power of your company if every employee could leverage the collective knowledge of everybody else, and if this collective knowledge could stay with your company and grow, even if individuals leave!*

Your company's ability to fully benefit from continuous permanent improvement would be incomplete unless you have a way of making relevant knowledge that people need to do their jobs available to them where they need it, when they need it, in a manner that they can use. Also, to the extent possible, can you convert the knowledge that is in your people's heads (we are talking of knowledge and skills that are relevant to your business) into your company's permanent organizational knowledge—and continually refresh and update it? Imagine how much more productive each of your employees would be if every one of them were able to leverage the collective knowledge and experience of the entire organization and not merely their own limited individual knowledge.

This is where *knowledge management* (KM) becomes relevant. This chapter talks about the 360-degree knowledge management model and our experiments implementing it in our businesses (Hariharan 2005).

## INTRODUCTION TO THE 360-DEGREE KNOWLEDGE MANAGEMENT MODEL

Try answering the following questions with regard to your company:

- Do I know what my most critical business processes are?
- Do I have a measurement system that helps me know how we are doing on these critical processes?
- Do I know what our customers think?
- Do I know who the experts are in my organization who can help improve our performance on each critical process?
- Do these experts form a closely knit community and constantly collaborate with each other?
- For each critical process, do we have a knowledge base that provides easy access at any time to all relevant internal and external knowledge that can help us improve our performance on that process?
- Do we effectively deploy the wealth of internal and external knowledge and expertise available to us to achieve maximum business results?
- Am I able to keep track of such deployment or application of my organization's collective knowledge and measure the impact of this on my top-priority business processes?
- For each critical business process, does the community of experts get *single-window* access to each other, and to internal measurement data, customer voice, and relevant internal and external knowledge or best practices that would together help them continuously improve performance on that process?

If your answer to *all* of the above questions is *yes*, you are among the minority of organizations worldwide that have a truly effective knowledge management system. If you answered *no* to some of these questions—particularly the last three questions—the 360-degree KM approach could help your organization. The objective of this chapter is to attempt to help your organization get maximum business results by adopting a 360-degree approach to KM.

After briefly touching on *what is KM* and *why KM*, the chapter primarily focuses on *how*. *How* to keep KM relevant to the business, *how* to keep your KM efforts focused, *how* to ensure real business results and performance improvements through KM, *how* KM really works, *how* to enable single-window (360-degree) access to *all* knowledge within and outside your organization that is relevant to your business, and *how* to organize this knowledge around your most critical business processes to enable your company to manage and improve its performance on these processes.

## *WHAT* IS KNOWLEDGE MANAGEMENT?

While KM has many definitions, for most business organizations, KM is what KM does—for business results and for creating an organizational culture of uninhibited sharing and replication of knowledge. KM is a tool to achieve business objectives better and faster—through an integrated set of initiatives, systems, and behavioral interventions—aimed at promoting smooth flow and sharing of knowledge relevant to your business, and elimination of reinvention.

## *WHY* KNOWLEDGE MANAGEMENT?

Knowledge management, effectively deployed, can be a powerful tool or enabler of:

1. Consistent customer experience by reducing variation in performance across time or across different geographies or units of your business
2. Speed in business results by eliminating reinvention
3. Empowering each individual employee to leverage the collective knowledge of the entire organization in serving customers
4. Converting individual knowledge into reusable organizational knowledge—to the extent possible

## THE SIX *HOW* QUESTIONS

For a majority of organizations worldwide, their definition of *what* they mean by KM and *why* they embarked upon a formal KM program would largely be as given above, though they may be worded differently. We now move on to the main theme of this chapter, which is *how*. We will try to answer the following questions:

1. *How* do we keep KM relevant to the business?
2. *How* do we focus our KM efforts and time to effectively deliver results in top-priority business areas rather than spread our resources too thin?
3. *How* do we ensure real business results and performance improvements through KM?
4. *How* does KM really work?
5. *How* do we enable single-window (360-degree) access to *all* knowledge within and outside our organization that is relevant to our business?
6. *How* do we organize this knowledge around our most critical business processes to enable our company to manage and improve its performance on these processes?

Start by identifying and defining a few vital processes that are most critical to your business. We will simply call these "top priority" processes. Usually, these tend to be processes that directly impact customers or revenue or cost. Make sure that you select a manageable number of processes. About five important processes is a good number to ensure that you are able to focus your KM efforts, time, and resources effectively and get real results quickly. You can always add more processes later, after your KM processes and culture have been established in the initial areas—which are, in any case, the most critical five processes of your business.

## COMMUNITIES OF EXPERTS AND KNOWLEDGE CHAMPIONS

Having identified your top-priority processes, create a *community of experts* around each process. Identify one of the experts as a *knowledge champion* for each community. Typically, a person who *owns* a business process would also be a knowledge champion for their process. Each community could have several experts, but it is critical to make only one person the knowledge champion. It is important that this person has high levels of expectations, buy-in, and enthusiasm with regard to your KM program. The knowledge champion must also have a stake in the success of the community, and in collaboration, sharing, and replication of knowledge among the members of their community (we're talking about knowledge that is specifically relevant to improving performance on their process). It is also important that the knowledge champion is suitably empowered to demand and get any necessary behavioral alignment from members of their community.

## ROLE OF KNOWLEDGE CHAMPIONS AND COMMUNITIES OF EXPERTS

The role of the knowledge champion and the community of experts is to form a pool of talent in their area of expertise and to ensure that this pool is available in its entirety to all parts of the organization. They must collaborate and promote knowledge sharing and replication in their area. The knowledge champion must *own* the knowledge repository for their process (more on repositories below).

## THE FIRST THREE *HOW* QUESTIONS HAVE BEEN ANSWERED

Thus far, we identified the top-priority business processes for our organization, created a community of experts for each process, and nominated an enthusiastic and empowered knowledge champion for each community, who has high expectations from their KM program. With this, we just finished answering the first three *how* questions: *how* to keep KM relevant to your business, *how* to keep your KM efforts focused, and *how* to ensure real business results and performance improvements through KM.

You might notice that we haven't even talked about technology or intranets or portals yet. Many companies, having invested heavily in sophisticated technology solutions for KM, have been disappointed at the results. The reason for this is that they jumped into the technology without answering the first three *how* questions.

## *HOW* KM REALLY WORKS

Actually, what KM does is disarmingly simple. All it does is provide the members of each community of experts (created around one of your top-priority business processes and including a knowledge champion) access to each other and to the repository of documented knowledge relevant to improving performance on their top-priority process. KM also makes each member of a community *want* to collaborate with the rest of their community and others, and *want* to promote a culture of sharing and replication of knowledge relevant to their community. In the initial phases of your KM program, they may *want* to do so because your organization may put in place some *motivational factors* to encourage this kind of behavior—perhaps it is part of their performance appraisal, or you have special rewards and recognition for knowledge sharing and replication.

> Actually, what KM does is disarmingly simple. All it does is provide the members of each community of experts (created around one of your top-priority business processes and including a knowledge champion) access to each other and to the repository of documented knowledge relevant to improving performance on their top-priority process.

As a community experiences faster results and improved performance on their top-priority process, you will find that they *want* to "do" KM anyway because it is helping them in their own jobs, whether you give them special rewards or not, whether KM is part of their performance appraisals or not, and whether you call it KM or not. A sure sign of the increasing KM maturity of your organization is that you will find that your formal KM program "evaporates," or gets embedded into your people's regular jobs and work processes. And when this maturity peaks, collaborative innovation, knowledge sharing, and replication become your organization's way of life—and reinvention and NIH (not invented here) get a richly deserved deathblow.

## THE 360-DEGREE KNOWLEDGE MANAGEMENT MODEL

The 360-degree approach to KM is about unleashing the combined power of knowledge and expertise from within and outside your organization along six interrelated dimensions for each of your top-priority business processes. 360-degree KM provides each knowledge champion and each expert single-window access to *all* knowledge and expertise from within and outside your organization that is relevant to their process. It enables your knowledge champions and experts to manage and improve performance on these processes better, faster, and with zero reinvention. And when each community does so, because your KM communities are organized around your most critical processes, your overall business performance is bound to improve.

## THE SIX DIMENSIONS OF 360-DEGREE KM

You can think of the 360-degree KM approach as a central core (representing a top-priority business process) with six circles around it. Each circle represents one knowledge dimension related to that process (see Figure 24). At the center or core of the 360-degree KM model are your top-priority business processes. For each top-priority process, 360-degree KM creates a *knowledge repository* in which is organized *all* relevant knowledge and expertise—that would be relevant to helping the knowledge champion and experts for that process improve performance on the process—under six *knowledge dimensions*.

*Dimension 1* is the community of experts itself, headed by the knowledge champion. This is the most critical dimension. This is the only one of the six dimensions that is a living dimension—the other five dimensions exist to aid this critical dimension. Dimension 1 ensures that each member of each community has easy access to the rest of their community, provides them facilities for collaboration, and knits them into a common pool of talent that is available to all parts of the organization. Communities of experts may also include experts from outside the organization.

*Dimension 2* for each community is the internal measurement system or dashboard for their top-priority process. This provides the knowledge champion and experts a view to how they are doing on their process, and helps them assess performance on their process across different business units, across time periods, and against benchmarks or targets. It helps them to understand where they are and where they need to go.

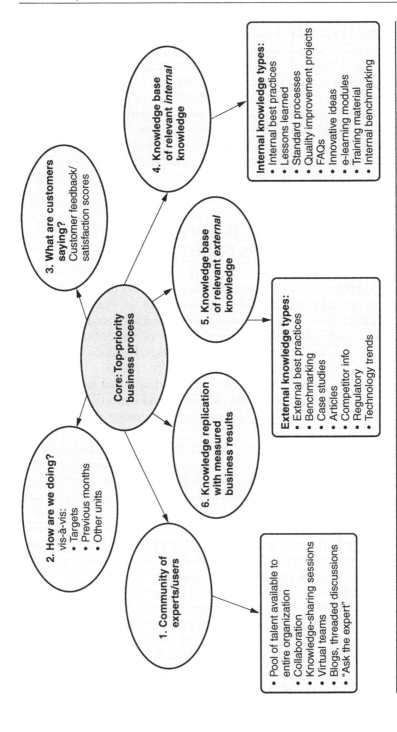

**Figure 24** The 360-degree knowledge management model.

*Dimension 3* is the voice of customers relevant to each top-priority process. Like many organizations, your company might have periodic customer satisfaction surveys. Perhaps you could identify one or a set of customer satisfaction indices from your customer satisfaction measurement system that are related to each of your top-priority internal processes. For example, for a service company that sends monthly bills to its customers, an internal measure could be the percentage of bills with errors. A related customer satisfaction index for this process could be the customer satisfaction score on accuracy of bills. You should be able to map each of your customer-impacting processes from your top-priority list with related customer satisfaction indices.

Dimensions 2 and 3 together ensure that your knowledge champions and experts get a balanced picture of their own internal measurements as well as what customers think.

*Dimension 4* is the knowledge base of all knowledge *internal* to your organization that could be useful in helping the knowledge champion and experts improve performance on their process. Internal knowledge could include best practices or lessons learned shared by employees, standard documented processes, quality improvement projects, innovative ideas, FAQs, internal benchmarking, e-learning modules, or training material.

*Dimension 5* is the knowledge base of all knowledge *external* to your organization that could be useful in helping the knowledge champion and experts improve performance on their process. Types of external knowledge could include external best practices or lessons learned, case studies, and information on markets, customers, competitors, the regulatory environment, or technology trends.

While *any* internal or external knowledge could be shared and published in your *repositories* of internal and external knowledge under dimensions 4 and 5, the key is to ensure that all knowledge that enters your knowledge base has some potential, if applied, to improve performance on the relevant business process. While all employees should be allowed to submit relevant internal or external knowledge to your knowledge base, a simple rule that must be followed by knowledge champions and experts before publishing a knowledge submission on their knowledge repository is to ask "Does this have some potential replication value? If this is applied, is there a potential to improve performance on my process?" If the answer is yes, they should go ahead and publish the knowledge submission.

Many organizations have a taxonomy or classification scheme to organize knowledge in their knowledge bases to facilitate easy search and retrieval. Having standard formats for documenting best practices, lessons learned, or case studies also helps to keep your content concise and replication-oriented.

## BALANCING RELEVANCE AND CONTENT QUALITY WITH CULTURE BUILDING

Knowledge champions and experts have a vital role to play in ensuring high-quality content in their knowledge bases, high rates of replication of published knowledge, and real business results from these replications. At the same time, they are also responsible for building a culture of knowledge sharing in the organization. They must handle this responsibility with maturity. In the initial stages of your KM program, knowledge champions and experts may be more liberal and accept most knowledge submissions in order to encourage more knowledge sharing across the organization. Once a culture of knowledge sharing is fairly established, the quality screws could be gradually tightened. Even then, any knowledge submission that can not be published must be handled sensitively, and it is the responsibility of the knowledge champion to ensure that the concerned employee continues contributing in future.

> *Knowledge champions and experts have a vital role to play in ensuring high-quality content in their knowledge bases, high rates of replication of published knowledge, and real business results from these replications.*

*Dimension 6* consists of all replications or applications of knowledge from your knowledge base that result in performance improvement in the relevant top-priority process—in other words, demonstrated business results. Just like internal and external knowledge, it is important to document (in a standard format) and publish each completed knowledge replication with demonstrated business results in the relevant knowledge repository. This calls for discipline—but this is critical for three reasons. First, it helps to capture the results of KM in terms of real business results—something that many companies struggle with. Second, documenting and publishing replications creates visibility and encourages more replications and more results. Third, hardly any replication is a 100 percent copy of an existing knowledge submission. Almost every knowledge replication would have used an existing knowledge submission as a base and then adapted, customized, or built upon it to meet the current requirement. In this process, new knowledge is added to the knowledge base. Thus, almost every replication not only brings business results, but also adds new knowledge to your knowledge base. KM is a never-ending *cycle*, and your organization's knowledge keeps growing each time knowledge is replicated.

## ESTABLISH STANDARD KM PROCESSES

The effectiveness of your 360-degree KM program in delivering real business results will go up exponentially if you establish standard processes for sharing and replication of knowledge. Do not leave submission and publication of knowledge in your knowledge repositories, and the deployment of your organization's knowledge assets, to chance. Put in place simple but robust processes that make it mandatory—not optional—to share internal best practices and other internal and external knowledge relevant to your top-priority processes. Likewise, put in place a process to close-loop every knowledge submission that is published in your knowledge bases. Business results of KM come only from replication—therefore, replication can not be a matter of choice or chance.

Eventually, as KM maturity increases, these processes will get embedded in your regular work processes.

## THE ROLE OF TECHNOLOGY IN 360-DEGREE KM

Company after company worldwide has learned the hard (and expensive) way—and in the process, ensured that it is now fairly well accepted—that KM is not about technology. The big challenges lie in top management conviction and seriousness, keeping KM relevant to the business, and in the people and culture arena.

> *Company after company worldwide has learned the hard (and expensive) way—and, in the process, ensured that it is now fairly well accepted—that KM is not about technology. The big challenges lie in top management conviction and seriousness, keeping KM relevant to the business, and in the people and culture arena.*

That said, there is no doubt that technology can play a vital enabling role in each of the six dimensions of 360-degree KM. Let us see how.

In dimension 1 (community of experts), technology can knit the experts together into a virtual community and aid collaboration. It can also help to provide the entire organization easy access to experts in each top-priority process through corporate yellow pages or similar tools. In dimension 2 (internal measurements) and dimension 3 (customer voice), most companies today use technology in some form for measurement and reporting. In dimensions 4, 5, and 6 (knowledge bases of internal knowledge, external knowledge, and replications), many companies use their intranet and KM portals to organize knowledge and provide search and retrieval capability. Finally, for each top-priority process, technology can effectively provide single-window access to knowledge and expertise in all six knowledge dimensions relevant to that process.

## EXAMPLES OF BUSINESS RESULTS FROM APPLICATION OF 360-DEGREE KM

Over the years, we had the opportunity to apply the 360-degree KM model at several businesses. Some examples of results are given below.

One company implemented 360-degree KM for their sales process. The "community of experts" in this case consists of nearly the entire sales team of about 400 employees. They use the KM platform as a common place to share relevant internal and external knowledge about the business. They share their success stories. When someone has a question or a problem, they throw it to the entire community (now each person has 400 experts at their disposal). All reports and information related to their business are available on their KM portal. According to the business head, "The team is collaborating like never before ever since we implemented 360-degree KM." In a one-year period from launch of 360-degree KM, the business reported a 5% improvement in "on-time" fulfillment of customers' orders.

Two companies reported fewer customer complaints, higher speed and accuracy in resolution of complaints, and higher customer satisfaction scores, while acknowledging that their 360-degree KM implementation around processes that impacted their customers made a significant contribution to these improvements.

Another company used 360-degree KM to increase the proportion of first time right (FTR) sales orders. In a 10-month period, FTR orders increased from 89% to 96%. In other words, orders requiring rework came down from 11% to 4%, resulting in customer satisfaction as well as reduced cost of rework.

Companies have also used the 360-degree KM approach to help their people, irrespective of geographical location, to collaborate, exchange information and ideas on market trends, and come up with successful new products.

## KNOWLEDGE-DOLLARS OR K-DOLLARS

In several companies, we used a points scheme similar to airline mileage points. An employee can earn points called knowledge-dollars or K-dollars every time she: (a) contributes a best practice or other relevant knowledge to the company's knowledge base, or (b) reuses or applies knowledge contributed by other employees to derive measurable benefits (in this scenario, both the employee who reuses the knowledge and the employee who originally contributed the knowledge are awarded K-dollars). Employees can then redeem their K-dollars for prizes. We found K-dollars to be a great way to create a bit of excitement for sharing and applying knowledge relevant to the business.

## CONCLUSION

This chapter attempts to provide a guide to organizations for getting the maximum real business results out of your KM program. It introduces the 360-degree KM model, which enables single-window access to *all* knowledge within and outside your organization that is relevant to the most critical aspects of your business, and shows how to organize this knowledge around your most critical business processes. Thus, 360-degree KM enables your company to maximize its effectiveness in managing and deploying knowledge relevant to improving its performance on these processes.

The chapter primarily focuses on trying to answer *how* questions about KM: *how* to keep KM relevant to your business, *how* to smartly focus your KM efforts, and *how* to ensure real business results and performance improvements through KM.

Not all the concepts introduced in this chapter are new. Most companies have internal performance measures and customer satisfaction indices. Many companies have KM systems with knowledge repositories. Some even have active communities of experts.

Unfortunately, in many companies, while all or most of this is available, they are disjointed and all over the place, present in bits and pieces, and sometimes not available where and when required most. No wonder most companies today suffer not from lack of knowledge, but from suboptimal ability to effectively deploy *all* available knowledge and expertise relevant to their top-priority business processes—resulting in non-attainment of their full potential in business performance.

> *Most companies today suffer not from lack of knowledge, but from suboptimal ability to effectively deploy* all *available knowledge and expertise relevant to their top-priority business processes—resulting in non-attainment of their full potential in business performance.*

The 360-degree KM model introduced in this chapter and the answers to the six *how* questions on KM are an attempt to help your organization unleash the power of integrating knowledge and expertise along the six knowledge dimensions for each of your top-priority business processes, and thereby help raise your business performance to its full potential.

# 17

# Do Business Excellence Models Help?

*Used in the right spirit, a business excellence model can give solidity to your business.*

Many companies around the world participate in the Baldrige (NIST 2010) or EFQM (EFQM 2014) quality awards. While these are globally known business excellence models, there are several other models followed in different countries. Many of these are modeled on either Baldrige or EFQM. Some companies customize one or more of the models available in the public domain to create their own model. These models tend to be a holistic combination of parameters or "criteria" that can be categorized into three broad areas—leadership, enablers, and results.

We created our own model. Figure 25 shows a summary of the model that we used in one group of companies—just as an example. You don't have to follow our model. You could follow one of the standard models or create one that suits your business.

Having worked over the years in a variety of businesses that followed different models, I have reached the conclusion that no model is superior to any other. What matters is that you select *a* model that best suits your business and culture, stick with it, and participate in the right "spirit" (more on spirit in a moment).

> *No model is superior to any other. What matters is that you select a model that best suits your business and culture, stick with it, and participate in the right "spirit."*

| Leadership reviews (250 points) | Points |
|---|---|
| a) Monthly quality dashboard review by CEO and leadership team | 100 |
| b) Monthly review of Lean Six Sigma projects by CEO | 100 |
| c) Monthly review by CEO of improvement actions from customer satisfaction survey | 50 |
| **2. Enablers (750 points)** | |
| a) Process compliance (measured through internal audit) | 100 |
| b) Risk management audit | 50 |
| c) Process implementation/compliance—mission-critical processes (verified through external audit) | 50 |
| d) ISO 9001 certification | 50 |
| e) Number of Lean Six Sigma projects completed | 100 |
| f) Number of ideas implemented with business results | 100 |
| g) Replication of best practices with business results | 100 |
| h) Automation of business processes or measurements that resulted in business benefits | 100 |
| i) Implementation of 360-degree knowledge management for critical business processes | 100 |
| **3. Business results (1500 points)** | |
| a) Revenue enhancement, cost savings, and process improvements through Lean Six Sigma | 300 |
| b) Revenue enhancement and cost savings through implementation of ideas | 300 |
| c) Results through synergy/collaboration among group businesses | 300 |
| d) Improvement in customer satisfaction scores | 300 |
| e) Business results: (revenue and profit) | 300 |
| **4. (a) Employee welfare; (b) Social responsibility (100 points)** | |
| **Total** | **2600** |
| Note: A minimum of 1200 points is required to qualify for the award | |

**Figure 25** Sample business excellence model.

Our experience in a group of businesses that has followed the model shown in Figure 25 for nearly eight years was that the attempt to win the award led the participating companies to long-term institutionalization of excellence, increasing customer satisfaction scores year after year, and sustained business results. We also found the model to be a fair predictor of medium- to long-term future financial performance. Companies that consistently scored higher on the model were also more successful and consistent in their revenue and profit growth in the long run, as compared to companies that scored lower.

A caveat that I would like to share from our experience is that genuinely following a business excellence model can give substantial strength to your business to withstand short-term ups and downs and build a solid institution, but this requires mobilization of the entire organization, particularly the senior leaders.

The spirit in which your company participates is of paramount importance. Many of these awards require an award application from participating companies. The application is typically a 75- to 80-page document that the company must complete, showing how they did during the year on the various parameters or criteria that the model consists of. I know a few companies that hired expert application writers. Unfortunately, in some companies, the application writer seemed to be the only person involved in pursuing the business excellence model. Needless to say, such companies get no benefit from participating in the award.

For our business excellence award, we did not follow the practice of asking for an application document from participating companies. The award criteria were announced to all the companies at the start of each year, and points were awarded on evidence of completion of the requirements for each criterion.

To sum up, a comprehensive business excellence model can give your business solidity in the medium to long term—provided you participate in the right spirit, are honest with yourself (don't claim things on the application that you haven't done), and stick with the model that you have chosen.

# 18
# A Word to Business Leaders

*Excellence is the business of the leader.*

I do not presume to preach to business leaders (CEOs and senior management). Having worked with a number of leaders in several companies over the years, however, I have observed that certain leaders are able to get bigger and more sustained results from business excellence and, for that matter, from their business. I have observed certain qualities in these leaders that seem to set them apart from others:

1. *Creating a legacy.* I found business leaders who achieved significant and sustained results through business excellence to be leaders who sought to create an enduring legacy, apart from leading their business to its immediate revenue and profit goals. It is not merely the short-term financial numbers, but the thought of creating a long-term legacy that such leaders seem to draw their motivation from.

> **I found business leaders who achieved significant and sustained results through business excellence to be leaders who sought to create an enduring legacy.**

2. *Expecting breakthrough results from excellence.* Leaders get the results that they *expect* from business excellence. It

is like a self-fulfilling prophecy. If the leader's expectations are low, naturally, their involvement in excellence will be low, leading to low results. The reverse is equally true. Leaders with high expectations know that it is worth spending their time on excellence, and this gives them results. As Henry Ford said, "Whether you think you can, or you think you can't—you're right."

3. *Treating excellence as a strategy and not a task.* For these leaders, excellence is a strategy to achieve sustained success in business—and not a task to be left to junior staff or consultants.

> **Excellence is a strategy to achieve sustained success in business—and not a task to be left to junior staff or consultants.**

4. *Involvement and reviews.* I have observed that leaders with high expectations of excellence get involved, primarily in the form of regular reviews and guidance to their teams engaged in excellence initiatives. I have had the pleasure of working with some leaders who haven't missed a single month of reviewing their company's customer- and quality-related performance dashboards and quality improvement projects for years. I have known one leader who would start his monthly business review with quality- and customer-related performance measures, even before looking at financial numbers such as revenue and profit. This sent a very powerful message to his team about what the leader's priority was. And this faith in excellence was not misplaced; this leader achieved bigger financial results than most others—consistently, year after year. These leaders also know *how* to review business excellence. Some tips on how to review quality projects are given in Figures 16 and 17.

5. *Knowing that quality is free, but poor quality can cost heavily.* I have come across a few business leaders who told me, "I'd love to have quality, but we can't afford it." They seemed to think that a business excellence program costs a lot of money. My experience over nearly 15 years

working with three large business groups is exactly the opposite (between them, these groups consist of more than 30 companies in diverse businesses, manufacturing as well as services). Quality cost us next to nothing, and paid for itself several times over. To calculate the *return on investment* in quality, we took the costs saved through excellence initiatives and divided them by the total *cost of quality* (this included the salary cost of employees in full-time quality roles, any costs incurred on consultants or training, and any cost of process improvements). The return on investment thus calculated was 16:1 in a three-year period in one group of companies, and 50:1 in a five-year period in another group! And, for this calculation, we have taken into account only the direct cost savings; we haven't even considered other benefits that we derived from quality, like revenue contribution, improvements in customer satisfaction, or reduction in defects. In fact, in the second group, it was estimated that revenue, as well as profit, for each of these five years were on an average about 20% higher because of the excellence initiatives than they would otherwise have been. Clearly, quality is the best investment we made. On the other hand, we experienced that the cost of *not* having quality (sometimes called the "cost of poor quality") could be heavy: rework, repairs, cost of resolving complaints, litigation costs when customers sue the company for poor quality, lost customers, reputation loss, and so on. For a shrewd business leader, the choice between a small investment in quality and the huge cost of poor quality should be an easy one!

> *Quality is the best investment we made.*
> *On the other hand, we experienced that the*
> *cost of not having quality (sometimes called*
> *the "cost of poor quality") could be heavy.*

6. *Making excellence a key part of performance appraisals.* Nothing sends a more powerful message about the leader's seriousness than making business excellence a part of people's performance appraisals and linking their growth

and bonuses to it. After all, if you are rewarding your people for doing their jobs, shouldn't you reward them a bit more for doing their jobs *well*? (By "well," I mean to your customers' satisfaction, or at a lower cost to the company, or right the first time with zero defects, or faster without compromising quality.) On the other hand, shouldn't you withdraw some rewards from people who may somehow manage to make their numbers, but at a higher cost to the company, or after causing pain to your customers, or after much rework? I have known leaders who achieve sustained results through excellence to make excellence part of the performance appraisal of everybody in the organization, beginning with senior management, and for all functions—be it sales or HR or operations or accounting or any other area.

> *If you are rewarding your people for doing their jobs, shouldn't you reward them a bit more for doing their jobs well? (By "well," I mean to your customers' satisfaction, or at a lower cost to the company, or right the first time with zero defects, or faster without compromising quality.)*

7. *Making senior people accountable for quality.* I noticed that the companies that achieved the biggest business results through quality were the ones where the business leader made senior people (typically people directly reporting to the CEO) accountable for quality in their respective areas. As we saw in an earlier chapter, quality is too important to be the job of only the "quality department." Everybody needs to be responsible for quality in their jobs and to their customers—and effective leaders enforce this.

8. *Helping everyone see things from the customer's perspective.* These leaders make themselves and their senior colleagues *accountable* for quality to the company's customers. And they help everybody in the organization see things from the customer's perspective rather than their own narrow departmental view.

9. *Putting the best people in quality roles.* I have observed that these leaders recognize the value of having a small set of people whose full-time job is to help the company to identify opportunities for continuous permanent improvement, and actually achieve these improvements. How can you afford to have anyone but your best performers in such an important role? These leaders, in fact, select and put their best performers in this role.

10. *Spreading the quality culture.* A practice that we tried and found useful was to involve, over a period of time, more and more people from all functions in quality projects or even as full-time quality team members. This helped to create and spread an organizational culture of data, analysis, waste consciousness, and continuous improvement.

11. *Investing in rewards and recognition.* Rewards and recognition, given in a visible way, play an important role in encouraging a culture of quality, customer focus, and continuous improvement. The role of rewards is especially important in the initial years, when the company embarks upon its excellence journey, in creating the desired culture. I have seen that these leaders make it a point to reward people who show exemplary customer focus or deliver high quality or help to make quality problems visible and solve them.

12. *Seeking consensus as far as possible, tough decisions otherwise.* Some CEOs seek the consensus of their top team for all major decisions. I have seen some companies that faced internal opposition at every step—for launching business excellence, for instituting a rewards program, for making quality problems visible, or for linking excellence with performance appraisals, to name a few. If you wait for consensus at every step, you may never be able to move forward. In nearly every company that has achieved significant success through excellence, the program has been driven with complete conviction and involvement by the business leader. I have seen that another quality of successful leaders is that they are prepared to make and stick with tough decisions when required. Too much democracy could at times slow down your business excellence program. Dissenting voices will die away as people experience the results for themselves. Push your

senior team into the deep end of the pool—they will quickly learn to swim. I have also seen that most of the opponents come around once they see that business excellence actually helps them get better results (and perhaps bonuses) in their own business or function. If some of them continue to remain cynical, well, read on.

13. *Weeding out the cynics.* Here, I quote the chairman of a company that is globally known for quality. This company is a preferred parts supplier to global car manufacturers across the world. The manufacturers prefer them because of their high quality standards. He said, "Every organization has a small minority of employees who are recognized as highly intelligent but who are also highly cynical of any strategic change initiative. Such people are a big threat to your business excellence program. Because of their intelligence, they wield considerable influence over their coworkers, and, because of their influence over others, their cynicism spreads rapidly to the rest of the people. In an atmosphere of cynicism and low expectations, your excellence program is bound to fail." He advises that the first step before launching any change initiative must be to weed out the intelligent cynics from your organization. In fact, according to him, that's one of the first things they did in his company when they started their business excellence program. Visionary leaders put people who are high on performance as well as enthusiasm in key business excellence roles. Such people will work as early adopters or role models for the rest of your organization.

---

*Visionary leaders put people who are high on performance as well as enthusiasm in key business excellence roles.*

---

14. *Successful leaders are not "helicopter" CEOs.* For most companies that have achieved competitive success through quality and customer satisfaction, excellence is a key strategic tool, and hence worth the CEO's time. I believe that the days of the "helicopter" CEO are over. Today, CEOs need to go into some detail personally. Today's

world is too competitive, and successful CEOs today are more hands-on and more willing to go into details. In my experience, leaders who have achieved significant results through excellence are the ones who go into some amount of detail themselves.

15. *Successful leaders don't say "business first, quality later."* We read in an earlier chapter about the sad end of a company whose leader said "business first, quality can wait." Successful leaders know that they need quality *first* (and always) to attract and keep their customers, and to *have* a business.

---

**Successful leaders know that they need quality first *(and always)* to attract and keep their customers, and to have a business.**

---

16. *Creating a culture of seeing problems as opportunities.* Without exception, I have noticed that leaders who achieved the biggest business results through excellence see customer complaints and defects as opportunities rather than problems. They encourage their people to make quality problems visible and get to the root cause so that the problem can be eliminated. They discourage employees from getting into blame games, and create a culture of root cause analysis and prevention of defects.

17. *Setting personal examples of waste consciousness and Lean thinking.* Another quality of successful leaders is that they set personal examples. I have seen such CEOs personally asking how to achieve even small improvements in processes, and personally practicing the frugality that they expect from their employees. In one group of businesses, for years, talking about cost reduction or waste was not very fashionable. Theirs was a "growth" culture (or so they thought), and nobody paid any attention to wasteful expenditure. All this changed when a new leader came to head the group. His personal example and belief in Lean and waste-consciousness made these fashionable in the same organization. Not surprisingly, the group made a profit for

the first time after this new leader took over, and has been profitable every year since.

18. *Outsourced processes can not be "out of scope" for quality.* Much of the work in companies I work with is outsourced. We realized that we may outsource some processes, but we continue to be accountable to customers. Outsourced processes can not be left "out of scope" or "outside our control." In fact, wherever it would help, we involved outsourced partners in our quality projects. This is only logical because our customers don't care if our internal processes are outsourced; they hold us accountable for quality and on-time delivery *anyway*.

> **Customers don't care if our internal processes are outsourced; they hold us accountable for quality and on-time delivery anyway.**

19. *Having a proactive strategy for retaining your quality talent.* We found employees who were trained and experienced in Lean, Six Sigma, and other quality methods to be in demand by other companies. We realized that the company needs a proactive retention strategy to retain these critical resources.

You may be able to think of a few more qualities or priorities that you, as a business leader, would bring to lead your organization to sustained business success through excellence. The message of this chapter is simple: the business leader is the biggest make-or-break factor that will determine whether your company will achieve breakthrough results through business excellence.

# 19
# A Word to Quality Professionals

*The best quality professionals are the customers.*

I do not claim to be qualified to advise quality professionals. However, having had an opportunity to work for many years in this field with reasonable results, and having made my share of mistakes, I have observed that certain qualities go into making a successful quality professional. I did not possess many of these qualities, and learned several lessons the hard way. I have listed these qualities below, in case you find them useful:

1. *Be a customer of your business, hire customers in the quality department.* I found that the easiest way (rather, the only way) to see things from the customer's perspective is to become a customer myself. What better way to experience the things that your customers have to endure and empathize with them? I found becoming a customer the easiest way to understand any business—provided one goes through most of the common experiences that an ordinary customer goes through in dealing with your company. I also found it useful to hire customers in the quality department; in fact, while hiring people, I give preference to candidates who are also customers. The next-best option is to make the employee become a customer as soon as they join the company. Putting oneself in the customer's shoes all the time is a trait that must come naturally if one is to be a successful quality professional. I believe that customers would make some of the best employees not only in quality, but in most other functions as well.

> *Putting oneself in the customer's shoes all the time is a trait that must come naturally if one is to be a successful quality professional. I believe that customers would make some of the best employees not only in quality, but in most other functions as well.*

2. *Help everyone to see things from the customer's perspective.* I realized that my primary responsibility as a quality professional was to help everyone in the company to think and see things "wing to wing" from the customer's perspective, and not from their limited "departmental" view (it goes without saying that I am expected to begin with myself). One business leader I worked with used to say, "I want the quality department to be the customer's representative sitting inside the company—we'll even pay you a salary for doing this!" However, there will be times when quality professionals face pressures to abandon this customer perspective (such as short-term business interests being in conflict with customer interests). In my experience, in the long run, it is the ones who never abandon the customer perspective, even under pressure, that emerge as successful quality professionals.

3. *Go to the gemba, observe, do, be "hands-on."* I quickly learned that quality is not an ivory tower job. To be successful, the quality person needs to constantly go to the *gemba*, or the place where actual work takes place (especially work that impacts customers), meet and listen to customers, distributors, salespeople, operations people, employees on the manufacturing floor—in short, the people who make your business run. Observe and even try your hand at doing the work that they do. I found that this helps the quality professional to come up with practical solutions to problems. Also, some of the best improvement ideas came from these people on the ground. We would have missed some of the most innovative and practical ideas if we hadn't spent time at the *gemba*.

> *Quality is not an ivory tower job. To be successful, the quality person needs to constantly go to the* gemba, *or the place where actual work takes place.*

4. *Ability to execute or implement.* I have come across a few "armchair philosophers" who became quality professionals. They would complain that nobody in the business "listened" to them. I have learned that one of the most important qualities needed to be successful in quality is the ability to *execute*. Very few people in the business will be interested in theories alone; the quality person needs to work with their colleagues in the business to *implement* what they preach.

5. *Institution-building skills.* In earlier chapters, we saw examples of the monthly quality dashboard review process, or the Lean Six Sigma initiative, or the IdeaExpress initiative. The biggest reason for the sustained results from these initiatives was that these were *institutionalized*. In the initial months, the quality person occasionally needed to push the business to sustain these practices, but today they have taken on a life of their own. Now nobody needs to tell these businesses that they need to review their quality dashboards, or do LSS projects, or listen to their people's ideas; these practices have been institutionalized. Of course, the business needs to feel the benefits from these initiatives for them to get institutionalized, and that is the responsibility of the quality person.

6. *Ability to build quality into processes.* My experience with defects and helping businesses in their prevention (through root cause analysis and mistake-proofing) taught me that a quality professional must be able to build quality into the process—in other words, help the business design or improve the process in such a way that, as far as possible, the process makes it *impossible* for a similar defect to happen in future, irrespective of who "does" the process.

7. *Be dogged.* One of the biggest lessons I have learned is that to be successful in quality, one has to be as dogged as, well, a *dog*! People (including senior managers, who don't report to you) will not always see things the way you see them, their priorities will be different, or the organization may simply not have a culture where people are comfortable making quality problems visible. To my mind, these are the challenges that make the quality professional's job interesting. It is the ones who can overcome these challenges successfully, and still take the organization along with them, who will ultimately emerge as successful quality professionals.

> *To be successful in quality, one has to be as dogged as, well, a dog!*

8. *Balance the short term and long term—inner and outer wheel.* One of the most common challenges I encounter in quality is the business's quest for short-term financial results, or day-to-day "fire fighting" (usually both). This could cause the business to relegate permanent improvement to the back burner while they focus on the immediate concerns. Unfortunately, in many companies, the short-term pressures never go away. Consequently, permanent improvement permanently remains on the back burner. This is a common grouse of quality professionals everywhere. I realized that as a quality professional, I could either sit and gripe about this or try and do something about it. I decided to see if I could do something. I found that there were several areas where quality initiatives could deliver quick hits, or results. In cultures where people need to see quick results to stay interested, it made immense sense to balance our long-term business excellence program with quick hits. In fact, wherever possible, we designed our business excellence program in such a way that, while having an overarching medium- to long-term goal and strategy of excellence, it was actually delivered in the form of a series of short-term hits or milestones. In an earlier chapter, we saw the metaphor of a slow-moving large outer wheel and faster-moving small inner wheels. The fast inner wheels actually help the outer wheel to turn. The only "inner wheels" to avoid are the ones that will harm the business and/or customers in the medium term.

9. *Understand and talk the language of the business.* The quality head at one company was trying to push through certain important improvements in one of their processes. Some gaps in the process had recently been identified through an audit. The quality head told the CEO and senior management team, "We must improve this process, or we may not successfully complete our ISO 9001 certification audit." Not surprisingly, the problem was not taken too seriously by the CEO and others. Why was this? The quality person here was not talking the language of the business. The process gap was a serious business risk that could cause financial losses and customer dissatisfaction, but instead of saying that, she spoke about the ISO 9001 audit. It goes without saying that the quality professional needs to be technically competent in the quality field, but the successful ones are

those who understand and talk the language of the business. They need to be able to translate the quality priorities into the language of the business.

> *The quality professional needs to be technically competent in the quality field, but the successful ones are those who understand and talk the language of the business. They need to be able to translate the quality priorities into the language of the business.*

10. *Don't marry a model.* Experience taught me that a quality professional can contribute infinitely more results to the business by *not* being a mere "model specialist"—be it Six Sigma or ISO 9001 or any other model. It is important for quality folks (including me) to remember that what the business requires is to be able to deliver consistent quality products and services to their customers, do this at as efficient a cost as possible, and continuously and permanently improve their ability to do this. *This* is the company's business. Quality professionals who can help the business to do this will always be valued. Six Sigma or ISO 9001 or Lean or a combination of methodologies are obviously useful, but not ends in themselves. As we saw in an earlier example, the quality person's job is not to help the company to get an ISO 9001 certificate or a high score on a business excellence model, but to help the business deliver real quality on the ground to their customers, consistently. To achieve this end, quality models and methodologies are useful *means*—but it is important not to confuse the means with the end. I have occasionally come across quality professionals who seem to be "married" to a particular model and make it a point to lampoon other models. So the Lean *sensei* scoffs at Six Sigma, and the Six Sigma Master Black Belt finds ISO 9001 laughable. I find this strange, because my actual experience in numerous businesses has been that *any* of these models can give results. If we understand and appreciate their underlying deeper message, we will find that all models have the same message: focus on the customer, and work toward continuously improving your processes and reducing defects or waste. We also found that these models can actually complement each other beautifully; for example, we have used Lean

and Six Sigma and ISO 9001 as a combination in many businesses, and the combination gave the businesses wonderful results. I realized how silly it was to get stuck on some ideological difference and to get into theoretical debates on how "my model is better than yours." The quality professional's job is to understand the underlying message and spirit of the various models, help their organization select *a* model (or a combination) that suits their culture and their business best, and then focus on helping the business achieve real results.

> *If we understand and appreciate their underlying deeper message, we will find that all models have the same message: focus on the customer, work toward continuously improving your processes and reducing defects or waste. We also found that these models can actually complement each other beautifully.*

11. *Don't try to cheat the model.* I have come across a few quality professionals who would try to demonstrate that their company was compliant with ISO 9001 or some business excellence model or show that some process was running at Six Sigma efficiency. At times, the compliance to ISO 9001 or other models would turn out to be "in letter, but not in spirit." Or the Six Sigma performance would be achieved by manipulating the definition of "defect"; for example, in many processes, we can show a higher performance level (on paper, not in the experience of the customer) by measuring only what happens inside our company and not looking at the process end to end from the customer's point of view. We have seen several examples of this in previous chapters. We saw that companies that do this only cheat themselves. After all, what is the use of Six Sigma performance on some internal dashboard if your customers are unhappy with your company and plan to take their business elsewhere?

> *What is the use of Six Sigma performance on some internal dashboard if your customers are unhappy with your company and plan to take their business elsewhere?*

12. *Don't show off technical knowledge.* It is self-evident that an experienced quality professional needs to have relevant technical knowledge and skills related to the subject, including statistical methods. However, I have seen a few quality experts with excellent technical knowledge who felt the need to impress their colleagues in the business by showing off their theoretical knowledge. The less intelligible they were to ordinary folks, the more important they felt. But they couldn't go very far because what the business needed was *application* of relevant (often simple) quality techniques that would help them solve real business problems and achieve real business results. Besides, quality is an influencing role; a successful quality person is one with whom other people in the organization like to work. And who would like to work with me if I brag about my knowledge?

13. *Help people to win.* I hate to say this, but I have seen a few extremely capable professionals who could not achieve much success because of a single flaw—they felt a need to show other people to be idiots in order to feel successful themselves. For a quality professional, this is a sure recipe for failure. Don't forget, you work through other people in the business. You succeed only if you can help *them* win. Work *with* them and not against them.

14. *Don't ask for an army.* One company had 100 people in its quality department. Surprisingly, the company continued to have quality problems and lose customers to the competition. What went wrong? In this company, quality was seen as the job of these 100 people only. The rest of the organization had nothing to do with quality. I believe a large quality department is not required in any company; it could actually be counterproductive, as in this example. What you need is a small team of passionate people. Everybody in the company needs to be responsible for quality in their own job and to their customer. A small but passionate quality team can be a catalyst to help the organization achieve this. To share my own experience, in two large groups of businesses that have achieved significant and sustained business results through quality, we had fewer than 25 people in full-time quality roles, in a group of nearly 20,000 people! An important responsibility of these 25 people was to help the remaining 19,975 people improve the quality of their work and deliver quality to their customers.

15. *Don't retrofit analysis.* Over the years, I have had the opportunity to review hundreds of quality improvement projects in several

companies. I have come across the occasional project where no data collection or analysis or use of any quality technique was evident in actually solving the problem, but some PowerPoint slides showing so-called data and analysis or application of tools were retrofitted after the event, just to impress the reviewer. Sometimes this is done in an attempt to win quality awards. In my experience, this neither gives the company any real benefit, nor even serves the limited purpose of winning any award or points because experienced reviewers or judges at such awards can usually sniff out such retrofitting in minutes.

16. *Passion.* Like any other job, people who achieve success as quality professionals tend to be passionate about their work. To be successful, a quality person must be passionate about customers and quality and problems and getting to their root. If you are to be the catalyst that will infect the rest of the organization with the quality bug, you'd better be passionate yourself.

> *If you are to be the catalyst that will infect the rest of the organization with the quality bug, you'd better be passionate yourself.*

17. *Don't get into analysis-paralysis.* We encountered the occasional quality project where the project leader deployed various statistical tools but was unable to translate all this analysis back into a solution that would help the business. They were not able to come back from the statistical world to the real world. We needed to remind them about what they learned during their training (Six Sigma training, for example, teaches this) about the need to "convert a business problem into a statistical problem" for ease of analysis *and*, on completion of their analysis, to "convert the statistical problem into a statistical solution," and finally to "convert the statistical solution into a business solution." Your project leaders may need help from people with domain knowledge of the business to keep the project close to the ground and to ensure that they do not get lost in the "*stat*osphere." What sets apart a successful project leader is the ability to identify the few tools that are most appropriate for each project, and then deploy these with real results. Initially, project leaders may need help from more-experienced quality team members to identify the most appropriate tools for each problem.

> *What sets apart a successful project leader is the ability to identify the few tools that are most appropriate for each project, and then deploy these with real results.*

18. *Help create a culture of seeing problems as opportunities.* It is the responsibility of the quality person to help the business leader create a culture where problems are seen as opportunities—a culture that encourages people to make quality problems visible and get to the root cause of the problem.

19. *Bring quality "down to earth."* I learned that it is not enough for quality professionals to limit quality to certificates (as in ISO 9001 or Six Sigma Black Belt certificates) or training programs. These enablers are important only to the extent that they contribute to real quality on the ground as experienced by your customers on a sustained basis.

20. *Give and share credit for results.* I realized that it is important for quality professionals to ensure that credit is clearly given to the concerned functional owners and the business head for results from quality initiatives.

21. *Influencing skills.* I believe that not even the best quality professional in the world can achieve any results by forcing people to "do quality." In my experience, the best way to influence colleagues who may not be convinced initially seems to be to work with them and help them achieve results in their own business or function—faster, better, and in a more sustained manner than before. Most people get convinced when they see the results for themselves, and are given credit for it.

22. *Strategic thinking.* While quality involves a lot of detail work, I discovered that it helps quality professionals to be able to think strategically. Quality happens at two equally important levels. One is at the operating level or the shop floor—this has to do with quality of products or processes or service—and the other is at the strategic level where quality can and should be an organization's biggest weapon for long-term competitive success. Quality leaders with strategic thinking can help businesses make quality their strategy.

23. *Cultivate the habit of "improve every day."* I found it very useful to ask myself every day whether I had helped the business

make at least one small but permanent improvement that day. Obviously, there were days when we weren't able to make any improvement, but I found it a useful practice to ask myself this question every day. In our experience, creating a culture where everyone in the organization thinks, "Have we made an improvement today?"—every day—gives bigger and more sustained business results than a few people using sophisticated quality tools.

> *Creating a culture where everyone in the organization thinks, "Have we made an improvement today?"—every day—gives bigger and more sustained business results than a few people using sophisticated quality tools.*

24. *An eye for detail.* We found innumerable improvement opportunities when we went into the details of a business process. We would have missed these opportunities if the eye for detail were missing. In my experience, it helps a quality professional especially to have an eye for detail.

25. *Be practical and result oriented.* I believe that the quality professional's job is not merely to lead their company to some theoretical ideal of quality (such as following a particular model or achieving some certification), but to help the company to keep their quality initiatives of practical relevance to their business and their customers and, by doing this, achieve sustained business results.

26. *Positive self-image.* If you are a quality professional, remember always that you are doing one of the most important jobs in the company. Have a positive self-image (without being arrogant, of course).

27. *Set high expectations and deliver on them.* I saw that, sometimes, businesses don't know what to expect from their business excellence program. It is the responsibility of quality professionals to set high expectations—and then help the organization to achieve them.

28. *While you're doing it, do it full-time.* I have seen some companies where the quality role is handled by somebody as a part-time responsibility along with another job such as operations or HR or

some other role. From what I have seen, this is a dilution of both roles. Every company needs *somebody* whose job is to help the company focus on opportunities for continuous permanent improvement. If the same person is also given some other job that involves transactional work (such as operations or customer care) or daily fire-fighting, obviously, the daily transactions and fires will take up their time and attention, and no permanent improvement will happen. If your company can have so many people who spend so much time fire-fighting, can't you afford to have a handful of people whose full-time job is to help your company *prevent* the fires in the first place? Prior experience in operations or customer service or even sales can be quite valuable to a quality professional, but while in the quality role, it is best to give it *all* your time and attention. The reverse is also true; people with quality experience can go back to a functional role after some time. In most cases, I have seen that they are able to do a better job than before because of the process, customer, data, and analysis orientation that the quality experience gives them.

> *Every company needs somebody whose job is to help the company focus on opportunities for continuous permanent improvement.*

I have covered most of the traits and behaviors that I believe, based on my experience, make a successful quality professional. If I have missed any, you may add them to the list. Quality professionals have a key role to play in business. Usually, it is in their own hands whether they wish to be at the periphery doing some bits-and-pieces work, or at the heart of your business, working on what impacts your customers and your business the most. It is your passion and your belief in quality and yourself that will determine this, more than anything else.

# 20
# A Word to Services

*If anything, quality is even more important in services.*

I once led a team of people from various service companies on a visit to Japan to observe and learn from Toyota's world-famous quality practices and systems. Frankly, some of them were quite skeptical before the visit: "We've got nothing in common. We are in a completely different industry. What could we possibly learn from a manufacturing company?" There is an abundance of books and other writings on quality with manufacturing examples. Also, many quality concepts have originated in a manufacturing context. Perhaps this is the reason that some people seem to think that Lean and other aspects of business excellence are relevant only in manufacturing.

However, our experience in numerous service companies shows that nothing could be farther from the truth. The opinion of the doubting colleagues changed after the visit. The same people identified and implemented several improvements in their service companies using the various techniques and philosophies of Lean learned from Toyota and other manufacturing companies. We found that, if anything, Lean and other quality principles are even more important for many service companies than for manufacturing. This is for two reasons. First, waste in a service setup can be more difficult to see (hence, more dangerous) than in manufacturing, though it may be costing the company heavily. Second, the need to "build quality into processes" is even higher in several services—as we will see in a moment.

> *If anything, Lean and other quality principles are even more important for many service companies than for manufacturing. This is for two reasons. First, waste in a service setup can be more difficult to see (hence, more dangerous) than in manufacturing, though it may be costing the company heavily. Second, the need to "build quality into processes" is even higher in several services.*

As Philip Crosby (1995) put it, "Because of this mentality [that quality is not relevant to services] the price of nonconformance in service operations is twice what it is in manufacturing."

Quality is even more critical in services. Let me explain why. If you were a manufacturer of televisions or cars or any other tangible product, you could, if you wanted, hire an army of "quality inspectors" who would "inspect" or "test" every television or car before it leaves your factory, and separate the good from the bad. This may not be the most economical way of ensuring quality, and many manufacturers are trying to make their processes so robust that they assure quality without needing an army of "inspectors." Some manufacturers reduce quality inspection to a random sample of parts or products produced in a batch. However, the fact remains that it is *possible* for manufacturers to do physical quality inspection.

Now cut to services. In many services like telecom or banking or hospitality, unlike manufacturing, there is usually no scope for any *quality inspection* or *testing* before every time their customers experience their services. A customer of a phone company gets good quality or bad quality every time they pick up their phone and make a call. It is not possible for the phone company to do a quality inspection every time the customer picks up the phone. Similarly, customers who interact with their bank or their hotel or their airline experience either good or bad quality. It is not possible for these companies to do a quality inspection every time their customer uses their service—even if the company *wanted* to do such a quality inspection.

The only option that service companies have is to build robust, repeatable processes that will enable them to deliver quality service *right the first time, every time* to their customers consistently.

In other words, the *only* option for such companies is to build quality into their processes, and continuously train and retrain their people to follow the standardized processes. This is what business excellence can help them do.

Of course, appropriate technology can be used to the extent that it helps to ensure that the standardized process is followed.

A challenge in services could be that some extra thinking and effort may be required to identify the right performance measures, to define *defects*, and to put in place reliable measurement systems to measure these, all of which could be more straightforward in manufacturing.

Also, do not forget that even in a manufacturing company, except for the actual production shop, most other activities are "services" anyway, for example, sales, billing, collections, customer service, purchasing, and so forth. Each of these services must deliver quality to their customers. According to Crosby (1995), "Everyone is in the service business." I have seen some manufacturing companies where the quality program is limited only to their factory. Other parts of the company are not involved in quality—and continue to be a big mess! For example, I visited a power company whose power-generation plant is regarded as one of the best in the world, thanks to their quality program. However, the same company's corporate office, billing, fault repair, customer service, and other departments are a breeding ground for waste, inefficient processes, and rework. This ridiculous situation exists in several manufacturing companies. Waste, defects, and opportunities for improvement can exist anywhere in a company, not just in production or operations. Can your company afford waste and rework just because the waste is not in your factory, but in your office?

---

*Even in a manufacturing company, except for the actual production shop, most other activities are "services" anyway, for example, sales, billing, collections, customer service, purchasing, and so forth.*

---

*Can your company afford waste and rework just because the waste is not in your factory, but in your office?*

---

If you are one of those who thought quality would not work in services, you only have to look at examples of leading service companies—many of them global names—that have successfully implemented excellence and benefited from it.

Several real-life examples of implementation and results of various aspects of business excellence given in this book are deliberately taken from services. This is because examples from manufacturing are relatively well known and much written about, and I felt that writing about service examples would help to remedy, to a small extent, the relative dearth of service examples that are written about.

So, if you are in a service business, waver no further; quality, Lean, and business excellence are as much for you as for Toyota and other manufacturers. Quality can be your key weapon for competitive success, just like some of the big names in quality from manufacturing.

# 21

# Summing Up: The Cycle of Continuous Permanent Improvement

*The cycle of improvement never ends, but your business improves every day!*

I have tried to condense the experiences and lessons learned over many years of working with a variety of companies in business excellence into this book. The cycle of continuous permanent improvement is depicted in Figure 26. The message of this book is summed up below:

1. We do not have a choice between business and excellence. There can be no business without excellence.
2. Have a clear business excellence strategy—aligned with your business strategy and priorities.
3. Quality is the responsibility of everybody in the company—especially the business leader and senior management.
4. Identify what processes your business needs—from the point of view of your customer.
5. Have standardized processes and performance measurements—so that you have a foundation or base for continuous improvement.
6. Create a culture of making quality problems visible—so that they can be solved and prevented. Do not stop until you reach the root cause and eliminate it.

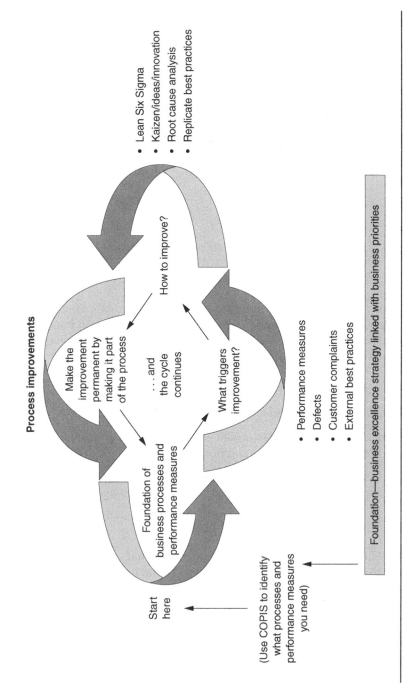

**Figure 26** The cycle of continuous permanent improvement.

7. Go to the *gemba* and walk your process as it happens. Observe and *listen* to people on the ground. This is the only way to identify waste, and opportunities to improve the process.

8. Most waste and rework can be avoided if you enable people in all functions—beginning with salespeople—to do their jobs right the first time.

9. A structured problem-solving method such as Six Sigma can help solve problems faster, and prevent them from recurring in future.

10. Lean and Six Sigma are as much management philosophies as they are methodologies or tool sets.

11. A complaining customer is doing a big favor. After all, they can merely walk out and take their business elsewhere. Listen to them and close the loop with them. Don't treat complaints as resolved until the customer says so.

12. Have a process of continuously generating and implementing ideas. Make innovation a process.

13. 360-degree knowledge management can help every individual employee leverage the combined knowledge and expertise of all your people, and convert individual knowledge of your people into permanent organizational knowledge that stays with your organization even after individuals leave.

14. A holistic business excellence model can give significant long-term, all-round strength to your business. It can help you balance short-term business results while simultaneously building the enablers required for long-term sustaining of the business and results.

15. The business leader is the biggest make-or-break factor that determines whether a company can derive breakthrough and sustained results and competitive edge by making excellence their key strategic weapon.

16. Quality professionals obviously play a key role and can add much value—provided they keep quality grounded and talk the language of the business. It helps greatly if your company's quality person is a customer.

17. Quality, Lean, and business excellence are as relevant (if not more relevant) in services as in manufacturing.
18. Continuous permanent improvement is a never-ending cycle that will help your business every day.

The next (concluding) chapter provides a path to getting started and implementing what we have talked about in this book so far.

# 22
# Call to Action

*The journey of a thousand miles begins with a single step.*

—Lao-Tzu

Let's now get started *doing* what's written in this book, in your organization. This chapter gives you a logical sequence of action steps that will help you to implement excellence in your business, no matter what your business may be.

1. *Create a clear quality strategy for your organization.* The first step is to create a strategy or framework for your quality or business excellence program that is aligned with your business strategy and priorities. This will help you ensure that your quality program will contribute to your strategic business objectives. Unfortunately, some companies neglect this all-important first step; these companies' quality programs can at best give them some operational improvements or cost savings for a short time, but no strategic, sustainable, long-term benefits. This step is primarily the responsibility of the CEO and the leadership team, perhaps facilitated by a quality professional who specifically has experience in helping companies align their business strategy and their quality strategy. It is a good idea to review (not necessarily revise) your quality strategy road map at least once a year to keep it always relevant to your medium-term business priorities. Chapters 1 and 2 will help you with this step.

2. *Define quality roles.* Everybody in the company—especially the business leader and senior management—has a role in quality.

Define these roles and make sure that people understand their roles. See Chapter 3.

3. *Identify what processes your business needs.* Create a "master list" of all important processes that your company needs to have. This step must precede mapping or documentation of individual processes; you need to know what processes your business needs in the first place before you document the steps in each process. Review your master list about once a year. It is possible that a process that was relevant a year or two ago has now become redundant, or a process that does not exist on your master list has now become relevant. Chapter 4 provides detailed guidelines on how to identify processes from the point of view of your customer.

4. *Put in place standardized business processes and performance measurements.* This is actually not one action but two, but they are so closely interlinked that I thought it best to put them together. This step involves mapping or documenting your business processes, identifying important performance measures, and putting measurement systems in place. These two (standardized processes and performance measurement) will give you the foundation for continuous improvement. Chapters 5 and 6 will help you with these. Review your processes and performance measures (again, about once a year is a reasonable frequency for most processes) to ensure that they always reflect your current business requirements. Many companies institute a practice of process-compliance audits (an ISO 9001 program can help) to help them assess whether their processes as documented are actually happening on the ground.

5. *Make quality problems visible.* If you have completed the steps so far, you have a good foundation for continuous improvement. The next step is to make quality problems visible so that they can be solved and prevented—in other words, so that improvement can happen. Chapters 7 and 8 talk about different techniques or methods that will help you to unearth quality problems. Along with the *techniques*, however, you will need to create a *culture* of making quality problems visible. It is this culture that will enable your organization to see quality problems not as problems to be hidden, but as improvement opportunities not to be missed. Obviously, identifying these opportunities is not a one-time step, but must be an ongoing activity.

6. *Quality project selection and prioritization.* Select and prioritize quality projects based on your business priorities. Chapter 10 talks about three types of quality projects, and how to prioritize

your quality projects. Most companies I helped do a formal project-selection exercise at least once a year (typically just before the beginning of the year; this helps them to prioritize projects that will contribute to achieving their business priorities for the coming year). That said, however, it is important to remember that you also need to have some projects that are identified and implemented with a medium- to long-term business strategic direction in mind. Some of these projects may not necessarily contribute to the next quarter's or even the next one year's immediate results, but have longer-term strategic importance. In addition, a few projects may be started at different times during the year, for example, if a business problem suddenly becomes visible that was not foreseen at the time of the formal annual project-selection exercise.

7. *Begin problem solving or improvement.* Next, you need to put in place an ongoing structured problem-solving approach such as a Lean Six Sigma program. It is important to train your people in the relevant tools and techniques that are best suited to your business, your quality problems, and your type of performance measurement data. In many types of industries, and particularly in services, relatively simpler tools can yield significant business benefits. On the other hand, the more advanced statistical tools are often more relevant in engineering or manufacturing (actual shop floor) contexts. Chapters 9 through 14 talk about some universally applicable problem-solving techniques and about how to resolve customer issues from the point of view of the customer. A Lean Six Sigma expert could help your company initially with the methodology or tools, and in training your people. However, it is important to remember that Lean Six Sigma is as much a management philosophy as a tool set. Your mind-set (whether you see Lean Six Sigma as your philosophy, or as a mere basket of tools) will make all the difference between your quality program giving you strategically significant and sustained business results, or merely some short-term benefits that can not be sustained.

> *Your mind-set (whether you see Lean Six Sigma as your philosophy, or as a mere basket of tools) will make all the difference between your quality program giving you strategically significant and sustained business results, or merely some short-term benefits that can not be sustained.*

| | Step 8: Manage ideas, innovation, and knowledge |
|---|---|
| Step 9: Institution of business excellence model | Step 7: Begin problem solving or improvement |
| | Step 6: Quality project selection and prioritization |
| | Step 5: Make quality problems visible |
| | Step 4: Put in place standardized business processes and performance measurements |
| | Step 3: Identify what processes your business needs |
| | Step 2: Define quality roles |
| | Step 1: Create a clear quality strategy for your organization |

Note: The above nine steps are not one-time activities, but ongoing, continuous, and repetitive activities. The sequence shown here is the recommended order in which they are first introduced. This will help ensure that your quality program does not get reduced to random, disjointed activities, but consists of clearly planned components that are woven together by your quality strategy.

**Figure 27** Strategic quality program implementation model.

8. *Managing ideas, innovation, and knowledge.* Parallel to a structured problem-solving or improvement program like Lean Six Sigma, create a program or process to manage ideas, innovation, and knowledge. Chapters 15 and 16 can help you with these.

9. *Institution of a business excellence model.* A holistic or broad-based business excellence model can help your organization to have a balanced focus on short-term business results as well as longer-term "enablers." See Chapter 17.

See Figure 27 for the *strategic quality program implementation model.*

# HOW TO USE THIS CALL TO ACTION LIST

If your company is beginning its excellence journey, you can follow the steps in the sequence just given in this chapter.

If your company already has a quality or excellence program, you should use this list of actions to assess what stage of the journey you are at. For steps that you have already covered, you could review the relevant chapters to see if there are any useful aspects that might help you to further strengthen or build upon what you already have, and then do the remaining steps.

If you have already embarked upon a certain step without doing a previous step, it may be worthwhile to pause for a moment and consider doing the missing step first, before you proceed. For example, if your company has already launched a Lean Six Sigma (LSS) program without creating a culture where people feel encouraged to make quality problems visible, you may not get full benefits from your LSS program. Some major quality problems may remain hidden, while your limited LSS resources may be getting spent on relatively minor issues.

If implemented effectively, these steps could help you derive full potential benefits from quality, and will help you make your quality program a significant contributor to achieving your strategic business priorities in a sustained manner.

## CONCLUSION

This book attempts to give you a holistic and strategic approach to quality, rather than the limited view that restricts the benefits to only certain operational or tactical aspects—(and even these benefits are often not sustainable). The difference is more in senior management's mind-set and philosophy toward quality, rather than in tools and techniques. Businesses where the leaders have succeeded in thus broadening their approach to quality have experienced significant and sustained business results; I have shared several examples of these throughout the book.

> *Businesses where the leaders have a holistic and strategic approach to quality—and not a limited tactical view—have experienced significant and sustained business results.*

In this book, I have tried to tell the story of business excellence without putting you to sleep—through actual experiences, examples, and anecdotes. The book mostly talks about firsthand experiences in implementing business excellence. I thought that this way you would find it more interesting and, more importantly, easier to implement in your organization. While there are numerous books on different aspects of quality or business excellence, I felt there was a need for a book that "puts it all together." I have tried to cover all aspects of excellence, from strategy and culture to implementation and measurement, to results and sustaining—and tried to put it in a logical flow. You can judge whether I have been able to do a reasonable job. Most importantly, I hope you found it fun to read and somewhat useful to implement. I would love to hear from you.

# References

asq.org. "Quality Function Deployment." Accessed 3/12/14. http://asq.org/learn-about-quality/qfd-quality-function-deployment/overview/overview.html.

Crosby, Philip B. 1995. *Quality without Tears*. New York: McGraw-Hill.

EFQM. 2014. EFQM home page. Accessed 3/13/14. http://www.efqm.org/.

Hariharan, Arun. 2005. "360 Degree Knowledge Management." *Journal of Knowledge Management Practice*, May. Accessed 3/13/14. www.tlainc.com/articl86.htm.

Kaplan, Robert S., and David P. Norton. 1992. "The Balanced Scorecard—Measures That Drive Performance." *Harvard Business Review*, January–February.

Liker, Jeffrey K. 2004. *The Toyota Way*. New York: McGraw-Hill.

NIST. 2010. Baldrige Program home page. Accessed 3/13/14. http://www.nist.gov/baldrige/index.cfm.

siliconfareast.com. 2004. "The 5 'S' Process: Seiri, Seiton, Seiso, Seiketsu, Shitsuke." Accessed 3/11/14. http://www.siliconfareast.com/5S.htm.

Welch, Jack. 2005. *Winning*. New York: HarperCollins.

# About the Author

Arun Hariharan is a business excellence practitioner with nearly three decades of international professional experience. He has helped several large companies in diverse industries achieve substantial and sustained business results and competitive edge through business excellence strategy and implementation. His forte is to help companies make excellence a key strategic differentiator. Companies where he has led business excellence have also achieved organizational transformation to usher a culture of quality and customer focus across the organization.

Arun is the founder and CEO of The CPI Coach (cpicoach.webs.com), a company that provides partnership, consulting, and training in business excellence and related areas. He is the former president–quality and knowledge management at Reliance Capital Ltd. (one of India's largest financial service groups). Previous positions he has held include senior vice president–quality and knowledge management at Bharti Airtel Ltd. (India's largest telecom company) and head of knowledge management at the RPG Group (a large, diverse conglomerate group). He has also worked as a senior consultant with Ernst & Young's global management consulting.

In all the companies where Arun has led business excellence, initiatives such as Lean Six Sigma and knowledge management are significant direct contributors to revenue, profits, shareholder-value creation, and customer satisfaction. Companies where he led business excellence have won numerous international awards and recognitions for their results from business excellence.

Arun is a sought-after speaker or chairperson at business excellence and knowledge management events across the world. Some of the Six Sigma and knowledge management initiatives led by Arun have been documented as case studies by several leading business schools.

Arun is the author of over 40 published papers and articles in leading international journals on quality leadership and knowledge management.

He can be contacted by e-mail at thecpicoach@gmail.com.

# Index

## A

analysis, retrofitting of, 207–8
analysis-paralysis, 208
andon, 83
audit, process-compliance, 56–57
automation, and standardized processes, 57
averages, as performance measures, 114

## B

balanced scorecard, 68
Baldrige quality award, 189
Barlow, Janelle, 123
batch processing, as waste, 91
Bharti Airtel, xx
big hairy audacious goal (BHAG), 7–8
boards
   as customer representative, 18
   responsibilities in business excellence, 18–20
   signs of organizations with progressive, 20–21
breakthrough results, 193–94
business excellence, xx, 10
   versus business first mind-set, 1–4, 199
   CEO's role in, 21–22
   as everybody's job, 23
   as part of performance appraisal, 195–96
   quality department's role in, 23–24
   responsibility for, 17–24
   results versus expectations, 22–23
   road map, 11–15
   as a strategy, 194
business excellence models, 205–6, 224
   utility of, 189–91
business first mind-set, versus excellence, 1–4, 199
business leaders, 193–200
business process mapping, 43–58
business processes, master list, from strategic COPIS, 39–41
business strategy, quality as, 5–15, 17

## C

Carroll, Lewis, 5
CEO (chief executive officer)
  role in business excellence, 21–22
  role in FTR, 106–7
community of experts, in knowledge management, 178–79
company culture, 161
  effect on innovation, 170–71
company image, FTR and, 102–3
complaints, customer. *See* customer complaints
consensus versus decision making, 197–98
continuous permanent improvement, xix–xxii
  cycle of, 217–20
  strategic COPIS as foundation for, 37–38
COPIS (customer–output–process–input–supplier), 25–28
  versus SIPOC, 27
cost-saving projects, 119–20
Crosby, Philip, 17
culture, company, 161
  effect on innovation, 170–71
customer complaints, 75
  bank example, 123–25
  resolution of, 127–31, 153–61
customer needs, identifying, 25–42
customer perspective, seeing things from, 196, 202
customer relationship management (CRM) systems, 127–31, 153
  beating the system, 130–31
customer satisfaction
  commandments (lessons learned), 158–61
  FTR and, 102

customers
  boards as representatives of, 18
  closing the loop with, 153–61
  director as representative of, 19
  identifying, 25–42
cynicism, eliminating, 198

## D

dashboard review, 67–68
decision making versus consensus, 197–98
Deming, W. Edwards, 59
director, as customer representative, 19
DMAIC (define–measure–analyze–improve–control) methodology, 109–11
DOWNTIMER, acronym for nine types of waste, 78–79
Drucker, Peter, 25

## E

EFQM quality award, 189
employees
  effect of improvement on, 171
  retaining quality talent, 200
excellence, business. *See* business excellence
expert communities, in knowledge management, 178–79

## F

failure mode analysis, 150–51
first pass yield, 98
first time right (FTR), 82, 91, 97–107
  applications of, 101
  and company image, 102–3

and cost of rework, 101–2
and customer satisfaction, 102
importance of, 97–99
responsibility for, 105
in sales, 99–100
five whys, 136–37
five whys and one how, 136–37
5S, 74
Ford, Henry, 53
FTR sale, definition, 100–101

## G

gemba, 55, 56, 89, 202
genchi genbutsu, 83
goals
    long-term, balancing with short-term results, 204
    and objectives, 6–8
Grandma Cakes example, 43–52, 53, 54, 55–58

## H

heijunka, 83, 91
"helicopter" CEOs, 22, 198–99

## I

IdeaExpress, 165–67, 168, 171–73
ideas
    managing, 224
    power of, 163–74
    sustaining supply of, 169–70
improvement
    and measurement, 72
    and process standardization, 43–58
innovation
    continuous process for, 168–69
    implementing, 223

    managing, 224
    process for large ideas, 167–68
    process for small ideas, 165–67
    versus standardized processes, 52–54
Innovation Council, 167–68
in-process measure, 63
input measure, 52, 63
    linking to outcomes in FTR, 106
insurance industry example, 60–67
inventory, as waste, 94

## J

jidoka, 83
just-in-time, 94

## K

kaizen, 83, 137, 168–74
K-dollars, 187
knowledge champions, in knowledge management, 178–79
knowledge management (KM), 175–88, 224
    balancing content with culture building in, 184–85
    establishing standard processes for, 185

## L

lagging indicators, 67
language of business, 204–5
Lao-Tzu, 221
leading indicators, 67
Lean methodology, 77–96
    effect on profits, 93–94

and root cause analysis, 149
in service industries, 94–95
in Six Sigma, 111, 115–17
Lean Six Sigma
versus kaizen, 163–64
projects
selecting and prioritizing, 120–21
three types of, 117–20
reporting results from, 115
legacy, creating, versus short-term goals, 193
long-term goals, balancing with short-term results, 204

## M

measurement, and improvement, 72
measures, relevant, 59–68
mistake-proofing, 51, 91, 140
morale, effect of improvement on, 171
muda (waste), 77
examples of reducing, 91–93
making visible, 88–90
nine types of, 78–79
multiskilling of employees, 92

## N

Nippon Life Insurance Company, xx
non-value-adding time, 88–90

## O

objectives, and goals, 6–8
Ohno, Taiichi, 43
operational COPIS, 27
output measure, 52, 63
linking to input measure in FTR, 106

outsourced processes, and quality program, 200

## P

Pareto analysis, 144–45
partnerships, in Lean methodology, 95
perfection, as a goal, xxi
performance appraisal, excellence as part of, 195–96
performance measures, 222
averages as, 114
keeping current, 35
layers of, 64–66, 67–68
relevant, 59–68
as source of improvements, 75
poka-yoke, 51, 91, 140
problems
making visible, 71–75, 90–91, 222
seeing as opportunities, 199, 209
problem solving, implementing, 223
process map, formats for, 54–55
process mapping, 43–58
Grandma Cakes example, 46–52
process measures, 9
process standardization, 222
Grandma Cakes example, 45–46
and improvement, 43–58
process-compliance audit, 56–57, 64
processes
keeping current, 35
identifying necessary, 222
master list, from strategic COPIS, 39–41
responsibility for documenting, 55–56

profits
  effect of FTR on, 103–4
  effect of Lean on, 93–94
project charter, 115
project completion report, 115
project execution/implementation, 203
project selection and prioritization, 222–23
pull system, 94

## Q

quality
  building into processes, 203, 213–15
  as business strategy, 5–15, 17
  cost of, versus cost of poor quality, 194–95
quality culture, spreading, 197
quality department, role in business excellence, 23–24
quality improvement projects, Lean Six Sigma, 118
quality models, choosing, 121
quality problems, making visible, 71–75, 90–91
quality professionals
  advice for, 201–11
  customers as, 201
  professional conduct, 207–11
quality project review, 112–14
quality project selection and prioritization, 222–23
quality roles
  defining, 221–22
  hiring best people for, 197
quality strategy, 221

## R

recognition and rewards, investing in, 197

Reliance Capital group, xx
resolved but not resolved (RBNR), 131
return on investment, in quality, 195
revenue, effect of FTR on, 103–4
revenue-enhancing projects, Lean Six Sigma, 118–19
rewards and recognition, investing in, 197
rework, cost of, FTR and, 101–2
road map, business excellence, 11–15
rolled throughput yield, 98
root cause analysis (RCA), 133–51
  air conditioning duct example, 133–36
  business results from, examples, 138–39
  critical success factors in, 139–48
  and Lean, 149
  tests of effectiveness of, 148–49

## S

sales
  first time right in, 99–100
  responsibility for FTR in, 105
sales productivity, impact of FTR on, 103–4
senior management
  accountability for quality, 196
  involvement in excellence initiatives, 194
  role in FTR, 106–7
  role in Lean, 77–78, 90–91
  setting personal examples of Lean, 199–200

service industries
  advice for, 213–16
  Lean methodology in, 94–95
Shingo, Shigeo, 1
short-term results, balancing with long-term goals, 204
SIPOC (supplier–input–process–output–customer), versus COPIS, 27
Six Sigma management philosophy, 109–22
  and Lean, 111, 115–17
standardization, process, and improvement, 43–58
standardized processes, 8
  versus innovation, 52–54
  reasons for, 54
strategic COPIS, 25–27, 27–28, 41–42
  application of, example, 29–35
  business benefits of, 38–39
  as foundation for continuous improvement, 37–38
  model and template, 29
  output of, 39–41
  relevance in new business, 35–37
strategic thinking, 209
strategy, business
  quality as, 5–15, 17, 221
  road map, 11–15

## T

360-degree knowledge management, 175–88
  business results from application of, 186–87
  model, 176–77, 180–81
  role of technology in, 185–86
  six dimensions of, 181–84
Toyota Motor Corporation, 145
  Lean principles learned from, 82–83
  quality philosophy, xix

## V

value, defining, 86–88
value stream mapping, sales order example, 83–86
value-adding time, 88–90

## W

waste (muda), 77
  examples of reducing, 91–93
  making visible, 88–90
  nine types of, 78–79
Welch, Jack, 109, 112
why-why method, 136–37
"wing-to-wing" thinking, need for, 57
Womack, James, 77